Contents

Dedication

IF YOU HAVE CANCER, are recovering from cancer, or if you're supporting a friend or family member with cancer, this book is for you. My hope is that my story and the intuitive practices I used in my own healing will offer you comfort, hope, and a new perspective.

The price of wisdom is above pearls.
—Job 28:18

PREFACE

THIS ISN'T A TECHNICAL BOOK about cancer, filled with medical information. I won't be discussing treatment options, new therapies, or research from the latest clinical trials.

Instead, this is a small book—a personal, and at times uncomfortably revealing story of my own experience with melanoma, and how I used my own practices of spiritual intuition and Divine connection to aid my healing.

I don't claim to speak for everyone who's had cancer, or even folks who've had melanoma. I certainly don't imagine everyone will see things my way.

This is just my story, small and particular, of my diagnosis of melanoma and the two surgeries required to remove it, and the many amazing miracles that happened along the way. Through this Divine passage I have been changed forever.

As you read this book, you will also discover a scattering of what I call The Messages—spiritual teachings I receive in writing, as is my practice. The sources for these particular messages are Divine guides; beings I am regularly in contact with who helped me understand and heal from my cancer experience. The guides are always with us, and you may find it interesting to read these writings.

This book also contains Seven Meditations I used to create healing in my own body during my cancer journey. These include meditations on:

- Overcoming anxiety and fear
- Tuning into the state of your body
- Receiving healing from Divine guides and angels
- Receiving support from departed loved ones
- Healing your body at a cellular level
- Shifting your vibration to gratitude and bliss
- Surrendering to the miracle of your Divine nature

I have placed these meditations at the end of the book, so they'll be easy to find and use. These are the same meditations I used in my own journey. You can do one of them, or all of them, in whatever order feels right to you—they are designed to show you how to use Divine energy to create healing in your own body. I also offer audio files for these meditations at **www.sarawiseman.com**

INTRODUCTION

ON A GLORIOUS AFTERNOON IN MAY, the kind of day when you can't help but feel elated from all that spring in the air, I flung open the windows in the house and began folding laundry.

I was happy enough to be doing this—of all household chores, folding laundry is my favorite. I like arranging the towels and my family's clothing into tidy squares, and then stacking them in perfect alignment. This is a task that lets the mind dream as the hands work, and I soon became infused with a sort of bliss: the open windows, the easy chore, the spring day, all created a joyous expansion in my heart.

And so it was I became entranced by this simple and repetitive task, fully connected to the Universe, when a knowing came to me out of nowhere—a voice that clearly and calmly stated: "One day you will be a cancer survivor."

In shock, I searched the room for the source of the voice, even as my heart pounded in response to the words. I did not have cancer—at least, not that I knew of. The melanoma that was about to take shape in my life had not yet revealed itself. Perhaps, it did not even yet exist.

Looking back, it's impossible to know.

On that spring day I felt perfectly healthy, and the idea of cancer was the furthest thing from my mind. And yet this voice foretold a different story—of a journey that was soon to come.

Book One

The Journey

Part One

Diagnosis

CHAPTER ONE

The Soul Decides

ONE SUNNY SATURDAY you're driving along, radio blasting, feeling fine. You're in the groove, hurtling happily through time and space to wherever it is you're headed, when suddenly, in a screech of tires and brakes, everything changes.

You find yourself crashed into the ditch, lured by some tricky flash of sunlight, with your car totaled and your body hurt and sirens wailing in the distance. And as you wait for help to arrive, fear floods your heart like a stain. Your entire Universe has flipped on its side, and suddenly you're looking at things from a completely different perspective.

That's what happened to me. Except I wasn't in a car.

I was in a hotel room. A posh one at that, paid for by my publisher. I've never seen so many fluffy white pillows piled up on one bed, or been privy to such crisp creasing of the sheets.

I was in Denver, promoting my latest book at an industry tradeshow, when my life first flipped over. I'd had a busy day of meeting and greeting, and now was dressing for a dinner with my publisher and a few other authors.

I was feeling good indeed, in this lovely hotel room where fluffy white towels seemed to reproduce at will. I'd just showered, and now my body was clad in one towel, my wet hair wrapped in another, and I twirled in front of the grand mirror in my room, happily thinking of the evening to come, when suddenly I spotted something on my shoulder.

It was like that car crash. One moment I was fine.

The next moment, I was most definitely not.

I stared at this funny mole on my shoulder, and I knew right then, things were about to go horribly wrong. "I have cancer," I heard my mind say to me, in a deep, gut twisting kind of way. And fear flooded in like a tsunami.

I stood there in my towels, gaping at this mole I'd never noticed before. It was brown black. Scabby. Weird. Like something that didn't belong on my body, like something that was not of me: a strange, dark, evil thing.

I have cancer, I repeated in my head, even as I dressed for dinner. And then more hopefully … *I will get rid of this cancer. I will get it removed immediately, when I get back from Denver. There's still time. I'll go to my doctor and get it removed, and all will be well.*

There's still time.

As I dressed for dinner, I worked to let my worries go. After all, I'd only just noticed this mole. Surely there was still time to change its course. Surely I could just head back home, have it removed, and the problem would be solved.

I headed out of my hotel room, confident this problem would go away.

But the Universe had a different plan.

♦ ♦ ♦ ♦

I'd been running on adrenaline. Not the healthy fight-or-flight response that kicks in when you face real danger, but the adrenal exhaustion that comes from keeping a schedule that's way too busy for way too long.

Crazy busy, some people call it. Looking back, I now see it as simply crazy.

Make no mistake: I love my work. But as the demands increased, I found myself doing way too much of it. In the past four years, I'd written four books and created four music albums. I'd produced numerous audio courses, hosted two weekly radio shows, and been a guest on many more. My client practice was booming. I worked weekdays, nights, and most weekends, traveling long hours in the car, and sometimes on planes. In the year preceding, I'd done 152 events of one kind or another.

Not to mention two of my four kids still lived at home, requiring all the care and attention teenagers need.

I kept this pace, driving myself faster and harder for nearly four years, but when the calendar slammed over into 2012, something shifted. I noticed I no longer felt well. I felt continually anxious, cranky, and overwhelmed. I was tired, and to my dismay, I found it was a kind of tired that extra sleep didn't fix. Taking a weekend off, or even a vacation, didn't help. I had a different kind of burnout.

I was tired in my soul.

And although I still didn't know it yet, this prolonged exposure to stress and adrenaline—this deep spiritual exhaustion—was about to have serious repercussions.

◆　◆　◆　◆

You'd think I'd have seen it coming, especially with what I do for a living. I'm an intuitive, or what some folks call a psychic. My intuitive abilities opened up after a near death experience in 2000; this was the kind of crisis that resulted in absolute transformation—a life change, and a spiritual shifting into a whole new awareness.

Since that time I've written books and taught thousands of folks who are in the process of opening up their own latent spirituality—the Divine intuition that lies within each of us. I use intuition every day to help my clients, as I psychically "see" what's ahead for them. This means I spend hours each day in prayer, meditation, intuitive trance, and in communication with angels, spirit guides, and the departed. I'm also a channel; that means I receive spiritual messages from guides in writing—you'll read some of those messages in this book; I've received hundreds of pages of these in my other books, *Writing the Divine* and *The Four Passages of the Heart*.

Exploring spiritual intuition and Divine connection is what I do, it's what I teach—it's how I live. It stands to reason, then, that I'd have the ability to look into my own life and see what was coming! Of course, I should have been able to see the mistakes I was making with my own energy levels and busyness. Except for some reason, I couldn't see it. Or, more truthfully ... I did see it.

I just didn't want to do anything about it.

I *liked* the heady thrill of my work: the non-stop pace of writing, teaching and training, spreading the word about intuition and how people can use it in their lives, teaching folks all over the world about the miracle of Divine connection.

I didn't *want* to slow down.

And so, even as my personality pushed me—literally compelled me—forward, my soul had decided enough was enough.

My soul had decided to take matters into its own hands.

CHAPTER 2

Divine Timing

TIMING IS EVERYTHING. Especially Divine timing.

In a normal world, I'd have gone to the doctor directly after my trip to Denver, and had this funny, strange, brown-black mole removed. In fact, I did make an appointment the day after I got back, set for mid-July.

However, I never made it to that appointment.

Instead, in July, my mom was taken by ambulance to a Seattle hospital, where she spent the next three days fighting for her life. Thus began what I now call my Summer of the Hospitals. No lounging at the community pool. No trips to the Oregon beach. No evenings on the deck on long summer nights where the sun never seems to set and the chirping of crickets fills the air.

Life as I knew it had suddenly disappeared.

My mom had acute kidney failure caused by a bad reaction to a blood clotting drug. She spent three days in ICU, then three weeks in the hospital, then three weeks in a rehabilitation facility.

I drove up and down the I-5 corridor, a five hour drive from where I live in Oregon to where she lived in Washington, as often as

I could. My brother, who lives in Seattle, did the bulk of the heavy lifting during her illness, and for this I will always be grateful.

Of course, I was crazy busy with work during this time: putting the last touches on one book and in middle of another; doing my client sessions non-stop. Even when I visited her in the hospital, I'd sneak away to write or do sessions while she slept. I set up shop in whatever quiet spot on the hospital campus I could find.

It is a horrible thing to witness one's mother hooked up to tubes and patched into a master board of whirring and light, the incessant pump and whooshing of the kidney machine, while her face got greyer and greyer, and her life force grew dimmer and dimmer.

Even after she made it out of ICU, even after she left the hospital, even the day she finally got home from the rehab center, with her brand new walker and clothes that didn't fit any more because she'd lost so much weight—even then when she was determined "recovered," there was a sense of fragility, the idea that anything could turn at any moment.

I would have liked more time to think about my mother's illness—to integrate what happened and why—but I didn't have that opportunity. My daughter was scheduled for scoliosis surgery that summer.

Thus, I canceled my mole removal appointment set for mid-July, and rescheduled it for late August.

Then, I spent six days living in a hospital room, while my youngest daughter, then twelve, had scoliosis surgery.

Now, this is no simple surgery. The procedure calls for eight or more hours under anesthesia. Next, my daughter would spend a full six days in the hospital, and then a month at home, before life began to resemble anything like normal: sitting, walking, moving, even driving short distances in a car. This surgery also required many bottles of painkillers: oxycodone, valium and more … every day, round the clock, for several months afterwards.

The good news is that my daughter emerged from this major surgery with two titanium rods in her back, her debilitating 63 degree curve corrected as much as possible, and three inches of extra height. She looked straight and lovely, and the surgery was a success.

The bad news was that during the following weeks, I spent so much time caring for her that I canceled my mole removal appointment reset for mid-August.

"I'll call back and reschedule," I told the doctor's assistant when I canceled yet again, "when things settle down."

CHAPTER 3

The Phone Call

As came to pass during the Summer of the Hospitals, I didn't get that weird mole on my shoulder removed in July, or in August, or even in September. The mole grew scabby, darker, and bigger ... but I figured I still had time.

Just a few more weeks, I thought. *Then I'll do it.*

What can it matter, anyway? I reasoned. *There's plenty of time.*

After that summer ended, the school year began with all its adjustments and schedule changes and homework. Still later in September, my partner, Dr. Steve Koc and I took a much needed break—we attended a sacred music festival in Ashland, Oregon, where the sun shone and music played, and we had the joy of meeting kindred spirits from all over the world.

So it wasn't until October that I finally made my appointment with my primary care physician and had that strange, funny mole removed. By then it had grown bigger, nearly black, and ominous, and I would be happy to have it gone.

This surgery doesn't cause much pain: a quick injection that stings for a moment, an uncomfortable sensation of numbness and tugging, and the horrible recognition of what has happened, whether you can feel it or not. My physician incised deep as protocol dictated, 3mm, and then she sent the mole off to the lab.

"Put a rush on that," she instructed the nurse. "So we won't have to wait."

"I knew it was a bad mole," I told her, as I climbed off the table with my shoulder stitched up and smarting. "I'm so glad that's done."

She nodded, and I forgot about it, and when the call came a few days later, I was still in bed. I saw the number on my phone and answered groggily.

"Your lab results are back," the nurse said, and then she waited a beat, as if trying to find the best way to tell me. "It's melanoma."

There was a roar in my ears as I tried to understand what she was saying.

It's melanoma.
Melanoma means cancer.
I have cancer.

"Oh, no," I said, or something like that. "Okay."

"I'm sorry," she said, and I knew this wasn't what she normally said when she called people to give them their lab results.

I'm sorry.
You have melanoma.
You have cancer.

Fear swelled in my heart, in a way I'd never felt it before: big, pulpy, grey. I was having trouble breathing, even as I discussed with her the next step: which dermatologist I would use, how soon the lab results could be forwarded.

I didn't know how to push fear back yet, how to release it. I only felt it rise, like a grey black cloud that filled my body, filled my mind, and would not abate.

CHAPTER 4

Diagnosis

I NEVER MADE IT TO THE DERMATOLOGIST. After my physician forwarded them the lab results, they didn't call back—which I mistakenly took to be a good sign.

"How bad could it be?" I said to Steve. "If it was really bad, they'd have called right away." And yet, even as I said this, my body knew it wasn't true. My mouth spouted off easy phrases: "I'm not worried;" "I'm sure it will be okay," but my body held different truth.

In fact, nothing that was to come surprised me. All of it seemed foretold, like a movie I'd already seen. The dermatologist never called; they'd already passed me off to the surgeon, and when I finally did reach them, they had no information for me at all, except "this is where we send our referrals," and "they'll be taking care of you."

For some reason, even though I knew in my gut what was happening, I choose to misinterpret everything. I somehow had the idea I'd be having a simple, in-office procedure. I'd go in, put on a gown, lie down on the office table, get a local anesthesia, and have more skin removed from my shoulder where the mole had been, all the while chatting to the surgeon about kids' schools or weather or whatever discussion we'd use to pass the time. I'd get stitched up and prescribed some pain meds, and be on my merry way.

This was sheer delusion. When I opened the door into his office lobby, a small room filled with every kind of *People* and *Sunset* and *US* magazine ever written, I was nervous. I wondered if it was going to hurt, if I'd cry, and if I'd be embarrassed at my own lack of courage, my lack of stoicism, my lack of fortitude.

But it was much worse than that.

◆　◆　◆　◆

I didn't get gowned. I just sat there in one of two consult chairs and waited. When my surgeon came in the room and began talking to me in a slow, measured tone, I realized things were going to be different than I'd thought, and I started to feel dizzy.

My surgeon was tall, younger than me, and had the ethnicity of someone who'd once hailed from the Midwest: Nordic, Germanic—much like me. He was bald—he either shaved his head for convenience or to show solidarity with his cancer patients. He was wearing dress clothes that day: a shirt and tie and dress slacks, although in other days he'd sometimes wear scrubs, which meant he'd just come from the operating room.

He was steady and clear, yet as he talked I had trouble hearing him. Sound rushed in and out of my ears, as if a Universal control knob was being turned up and down, up and down, so his words made no sense:

Cancer.
Metastasis.
Tricky.
Melanoma.
Surgery.
Outcome.
Serious.
Mortality.
Concern.

That's about what I heard.

I strained forward in my chair, trying to make sense of it: I had melanoma and it had spread to a depth that was unsafe, so we couldn't simply remove more skin and call it a day. We'd have to go much further.

We'd have to make sure this melanoma—one of the deadliest forms of cancer—had not metastasized to any other of the many places it often did: my armpit, which might take it into my lungs, heart or other major body systems; my neck, in which the surgery was too complicated to do in town; or my groin, which was the same situation as my armpit.

"Are we going to do the surgery today?" I finally asked him.

At this point, he looked at me with complete understanding of my shock, confusion, and inability to process what he was saying at this moment.

"Not today," he said kindly. "We'll need to schedule that."

I have a funny kind of mind: I can take in copious facts and detail and spew it all back, while at the same time having such a complicated emotional response that I hear nothing.

This was what happened that day in his office.

Hearing nothing at the first visit is common, he'd tell me later.

And yet during this moment of extreme disassociation, I did not experience a silent screaming of resistance or fear inside my mind. There was no internal howling of "nooooo" that I've often felt when facing situations that are dangerous to me, or threatening.

I was afraid, but I also felt calm. A strange, weird calm I knew I could trust—even though it made no sense at all to trust it.

Melanoma.

Metastasis.

Dangerous.

Mortality.

Nothing I was hearing pointed toward trust. And yet my breathing stayed relaxed, and I found myself actually twisting in my chair, turning to look over my shoulder several times, as if to find the other poor soul who must surely be in the room with me, receiving this awful news.

He can't be talking to me, I heard myself think. *This isn't my story.*

Except, of course, it was.

CHAPTER 5

Mortality

THE TRICKY THING ABOUT MELANOMA, my surgeon explained, is how it spreads. This is what makes it so extremely dangerous: it's sneaky, fast, and spreads everywhere. I flashed immediately to a high school biology class decades ago, when I'd learned about cancer for the first time. Even then, I'd been shaken to learn of these evil cells that went crazy, suddenly dividing at an exponentially fast rate, dividing and conquering until they killed the body like a parasite kills a host. Which is of course, what cancer does.

Except, cancer isn't evil.

Cancer isn't bad—and it isn't good either. It just is. One day, we may find our research into cancer's ability to metastasize may help us create new ways of boosting cell growth for cells we *want* to spread quickly. Perhaps our study of cancer will help us solve even bigger concerns, later.

We don't know yet.

Yes, cancer can be tragic, painful, and horrid. But evil? No. When we see a tree overgrown with lichen, we don't imagine the lichen is evil, even as we know that lichen is killing the tree.

The tree is part of the process. It's in the process of dying, decomposing, disintegrating, and will one day be used as humus for the new tree seedlings that are sprouting around it in the earth.

Our bodies are the same. We're dying from the moment we're born. If you are a human, there is no immunity to this.

In the way we look at death in the modern world, there's not much to support the idea of our bodies decomposing in order to enrich the soil. In most first world countries, the body doesn't return to the soil at all—we're interred in caskets, or burnt into a fine dust of bone and ash, scattered or urned, as our survivors dictate.

But we do die, and at the very moment of our death, new souls are arriving onto earth. It's a heady passage, this time between times, and crowded with activity—a continuous stream of souls departing, while a continuous stream of souls arrives.

I don't know what you believe, but this is how I see it.

Time between times, life between lives, heaven, bardo, other realms; we have all kinds of names from different spiritual belief systems that describe this place where we go when our bodies are finished in this lifetime.

Beyond the veil, others call it, and this is a veil I actively envision in my intuitive work; it's a palpable thing, a portal through which entities may pass to and fro. The idea of separation—that we in this reality are separate from those who've passed—is all a myth. This information is what I knew and practiced, and as it all came flashing back to me, I hoped it would serve me now.

◆　◆　◆　◆

As I faced surgery, my surgeon explained exactly what he'd do, and why. The skin would be taken off the arm, to a depth that would provide a safe margin—a deep cut, and long—I'd have a big scar on my arm, about eight inches across.

In addition, they'd also need to check the path of metastasis, to see if the cancer had spread to other parts of my body. They'd do this by tracking the drain path from the original mole site—the natural course of where the blood and lymph traveled first, from that mole site.

This all sounded terrible.

I gritted my teeth and signed the release form.

"I don't want to die," I told him. "But at the same time, I know that I might. This surgery is the best choice I have right now. It's not a great choice, but it's the option that's here."

He started to say something, but for some reason he stopped.

I scribbled my signature on the release form, and we moved forward.

CHAPTER 6

Tsunami

WHEN I WAS EIGHT YEARS OLD, I lived by the ocean. My father worked in Hawaii each summer and so my mother and brother and I accompanied him, usually staying in a tiny rental house a few blocks from the beach, or sometimes in an old-style hotel on the beach—the kind you don't see much anymore. We did this for years, from about the time I was four through my high school years.

Hawaii sounds idyllic—enchanted and wonderful—and in almost every way, it was.

I spent hours each day on the beach, and learned to swim and boogie board like a native. When I wasn't swimming I was still outside: climbing palm trees, or collecting plumeria to string into leis.

During that month each summer, my hair quickly lightened from its usual reddish hue to blond; streaked and stiffened from so much salt and sea. My skin changed too ... I didn't tan, like everyone else on the beach. Instead, being a red head, I burned.

My skin turned lobster red every time I stayed out too long or forgot to wear a T-shirt over my bathing suit. It peeled off in giant sheets from my back and shoulders, and from the entire plane of my nose.

Not that I wasn't cautious, but at that time we didn't know what damage the sun could cause. This was before SPF and sun screens: this was an era when people actually sat out in the sun with foil frames held to their faces, or slathered baby oil all over their bodies, literally roasting their skin in the sun.

During those summers in Hawaii, my dad often got off work early and took me swimming. I have old photos of me holding tight to him with waist high waves crashing and frothing all around. On a beach filled with darkly tanned locals, the photos show clearly how I stand out: zinc oxide is slathered on my nose, and I'm the only one wearing a T-shirt in the water. Even with the limited knowledge at the time, I was trying to keep from getting burned.

◆ ◆ ◆ ◆

My dad died of cancer 12 years ago. Although by the time it was discovered his cancer had spread too far to pinpoint exactly how it started, his doctors believe he had melanoma.

Both my father and I fall into the category of people who are most susceptible to melanoma: fair skinned, red headed. His eyes were hazel; mine are blue. We both spent long hours in the intense Hawaiian sun every year for decades, another strong risk indicator.

I find it hard to realize that during those summers when we were having so much fun at the beach: laughing in the waves, screaming with excitement at the undertow and the next wave to come—those joyous, amazing times of my childhood and youth—that we were probably both getting sun damage that would lead each of us to cancer.

I also had difficulty accepting the fact that I now had the same disease my father had—and he'd only lived two years after his cancer was discovered.

I didn't want to die like that. In fact, I didn't want to die.

And yet every time I began to think about melanoma, I immediately remembered my dad … and my mind would spiral into fear and negativity. Every time I thought of my dad and his end, I descended into what I might call pessimism, or depression, or a pervasive sense of doom … as in, "What's the use? " or "I can't survive" or "I'm sure I'll die."

I spiraled right down into worst-case scenario and refused to budge. This vibration brought with it neither fear, nor panic, nor anxiety. Instead, I was enveloped by a great wrenching sadness—an absolute understanding of my mortality as fact, as reality.

♦ ♦ ♦ ♦

In cancer, and in other diseases, it's generally accepted that the way to stay into high vibration, the way to best allow the possibility of health and healing, is to disallow all thoughts of fear, sadness, and pessimism. To "go positive" as it were, and never allow a negative thought to enter the mind.

I understand the reasoning behind this outlook. And yet, I found something quite different in my own experience: That you could *push away fear*, by deciding you had the courage to face whatever happened, regardless of outcome. I would learn how to do that, and I did.

I could not, however, push away *sadness* in the same way. I could not push away sadness, because first I had to go through it.

It may be different for you. But for me, no matter how I tried to be happy, upbeat, positive, and maintain an affirmative attitude that "everything is going to be okay," when I faced the reality of cancer, I felt myself sliding into another place. My true thoughts at that time were this:

What if I wasn't okay?

What if I did die?

What if the cancer had spread, like my dad's cancer?

What if I wasn't going to be cured?

Once I started down this road, the worst-case scenario road, the bigger waves of sadness arrived:

I wasn't ready to go.
I hadn't finished my life's work—I'd only just gotten started.
I had so many things I still wanted to do.

And then, giant tsunamis of grief:
How could I leave my children?
How could I say goodbye to my partner?
What about the rest of my family and friends?
Who would care for my youngest daughter, who'd just had her surgery?
How would my older children survive?
How would my partner survive?
How could I survive the pain of leaving them?

I didn't want to leave my children; I didn't want to miss them, I didn't want them to miss me. I wanted to stay alive, whole, and healthy, so I could continue to enjoy our lives together. I wanted to be a mom, I wanted to help my kids grow into lovely adults. Not just young adults either, but full-grown adults with lives and loves of their own. I wanted to stick around and help them make their way.

And my partner? I could not imagine leaving him. I'd waited so long to find him, and we'd only been together eight years. I wanted decades more. I had so much to say and do and experience with him; I was not done with him, at all.

With fear and sadness, I faced the journey to come.

CHAPTER 7

Disclosure

SOMETHING ABOUT MY SURGEON'S YOUTH, his calm, and the unwavering air of sympathy that shone out from him took me to my next step.

This step felt risky; it was something I don't normally do outside my circle of clients and kindred spirits I work with, teach, and write for. In my world, mostly everyone is an intuitive, healer, or spiritual teacher—either already, or on the path. But in the real world—the mainstream world—I've learned to keep mum.

In the real world, I've learned to be private about what I do. I may talk candidly on my radio shows about my intuitive and spiritual experiences, because I know the listeners are on board with my belief system, but when it comes to the people I run into day to day, I do not readily share information about my mystical and spiritual experiences. I've learned the hard way that my views are not acceptable to most people.

Thus, I sized up my surgeon carefully before I decided to disclose who I really was. In the end, his sympathy convinced me to share my perspective; I knew that regardless of whether our belief systems meshed, he wanted to help me. I also understood he could do his job better if he knew what made me tick.

And so, I confessed to him who I really was: not as I might be perceived on the surface as woman, mother, cancer patient—but who I really was.

The first words felt funny coming out of my mouth, but I said them anyway:

Intuition.

Spiritual.

Mystic.

Divine.

Energy.

Vibration.

Intention.

Miracle.

If I had melanoma—which I did—I was going to approach the disease with all the tools at my disposal. That meant traditional medicine and holistic medicine. But even more so, it meant the kind of healing I knew how to do—the healing I could facilitate by entering into Divine connection and working with my guides and angels, and the energy of the Universe.

And so I told him ... carefully, cautiously.

About the work I did, the faith I had—not in traditional religion, but in my own way of looking at the Universe/God/All/One. I told him about the many miracles I had already experienced in my own life, and I told him of my firm intention to use all my intuitive and spiritual abilities to create healing in my body.

Regardless of what he thought, my surgeon didn't disagree. He simply held to his own course: science with compassion. It shook me to realize that his view, the medical view, wasn't as positive as my spiritual outlook. His view was all about using the research, following protocol, and then seeing what happened. His world was about statistics and outcomes, which in my case, weren't promising.

Divine healing wasn't a language he spoke.

This was a man who'd operated on thousands of patients and seen thousands of outcomes—some good, many bad. He had a different outlook than mine, devoid of the fierce, inexplicable faith in the Divine that permeated my understanding.

He was science based, medical, and neutral—he didn't know what would happen to me yet and wasn't about to make a guess. We'd have to wait and see. He was a kind man, and this wasn't personal.

He'd seen a lot of patients. Some had survived. Some had not. He didn't know me well enough, yet, to know which kind of patient I would turn out to be.

I found myself trembling with cold as I realized that, in truth, I didn't know either.

♦ ♦ ♦ ♦

The lessons you were going to learn hadn't made their way into your life yet. You scoffed at them. You rejected them. You thought they were silly, or made up, or not real.

You accepted some of what we provided to you ... the things you wanted to believe. The ideas that made you uncomfortable, you skipped or disallowed.

Your soul took this opportunity to experience the disease of cancer, because you wanted to understand the deep compassion that came from undergoing this experience—at some level, you knew this.

But what you didn't know, and what your soul had agreed to do, in triplicate, with full soul signatures (laughter) was that there would be more for you to learn.

Consider it as further university for the soul.

You didn't understand this going in. You're still processing it now.

These are ways in which a soul chooses to live each lifetime. As a new soul, as a soul who has not been here so many times already, you were ready to learn.

You asked for this. Not all do.

You asked for this as a challenge, and this challenge was readily provided to you.

The more who understand this, the more who are able to see their own mortality, to face this fear and still go on ... this is one of the lessons of all souls.

Even now, with all your experiences and your ability to move within the realms, you are just beginning to understand this.

Theory is one thing. Teaching is another. This time, in this lesson you were learning, you needed to understand it in your own body, for your own soul.

Fear was your first lesson. Even now, you still slip sideways in your understanding. Even now, you struggle to hold vibration. This is a life lesson for you; a great challenge for your personality.

—The Messages

CHAPTER 8

Fear

You learn a lot of stuff when you have cancer—there is much information to absorb, and you must learn quickly: the details of your disease, your stage, your treatment options, your survival rate, all the ins and outs of every kind of traditional or holistic treatment available to you, and how they often don't agree.

And yet, none of it means a thing until you've learned the first lesson.

Cancer isn't the enemy.

Fear is.

When you're faced with what to do about this disease in your body, this strange and aggressive metastasis of cells—there is no room for fear.

That doesn't mean you won't have days or moments when you're panicked, terrified, uncertain, and unnerved. What it does mean is that in order to see clearly, in order to work in the best possible way on behalf of your body and your healing, you've got to push that fear away.

Disallow it.

Banish it.

Move forward in a new vibration.

If you can't stay out of fear, it doesn't mean you'll succumb to cancer.

If you're courageous, it doesn't mean your cancer will be healed.

But I do believe that if you lose the fear, push it away, and ban it forever, you will rise to a new place in your vibration where you can create and sustain a new kind of emotional healing, physical healing, or both.

At least that was my theory.

Thus, one of the first things I had to learn from cancer, is that fear would not serve me. It wouldn't—it couldn't—take me where I wanted to go, and that the way to heal myself—either my emotions or my body or both, was to drag my mind out of panic, anxiety, and the edginess of fear and its incessant looping into lower vibration of thought.

Fear is like a galloping horse—once you let fear have its head, you'll find it's nearly impossible to get control of it again. When you get tired, when you feel sick, when you feel uncomfortable, when you experience pain … all things that happen when you have cancer … fear wants to run, away and further away, faster and harder and without thought of where it's taking you.

It just wants to run.

Another thing about fear? It's the opposite of trust. Fear is the opposite of believing the Universe is on your side, that you are held in the love of Divine/One/All at all times, and that miracles are a given, every single day.

Fear is about allowing yourself to think you're separate, though of course this is an illusion. It's about allowing your mind and body to sink into the lower vibrations: fear, pain, hurt, rage, and anger. All of these vibrations are of no use when you're trying to heal.

◆　◆　◆　◆

The first lesson you faced was fear. When you came out of the surgeon's office, you noticed the air around you was shimmering with a new sort of vibration, a vibration you do not usually exist in. It was a mixed vibration, and a confused one: part elation, which is a shimmering of what you might call blue, white, sparkling, effervescent. A high vibration, in fact the highest vibration you use in order to contact us. But also, woven into this was a vibration you sometimes descend into, have descended into during your life: a grey black vibration that contained all the fear, anxiety and anguish of the Universe.

The Universe always exists in energetic balance. Thus the higher vibration and lower vibrations continue to play out in a way so that summation balance is held. This means they can exist simultaneously and at all times.

For you, this began to happen in your body: the heights of passion and depths of despair both beginning to run a vibration system in your body, often simultaneously—at once.

This was new, and too much for you to manage.

Fear, the lower vibration, began to resonate in your whole body. This is why you don't remember so many things about your illness: even that first drive back from the surgeon's office. It's confusing to you. There were angels everywhere for you: the people on the street, the sidewalk, even the way the turnstile in the parking lot opened so gracefully, in love.

And you did notice the beauty, the incredible presence of grace in everything as you drove on the long country roads home; you did notice this: The clouded sky; the trees overhung with rain; the wet pavement.

But most of it, you couldn't see. You'd gone into fear spiral, and as we watched, it was clear this would be your challenge, your first lesson, and your first knowing. Fear, especially, brings with it the emotion of energy. In the human body, it is fight or flight.

For you, you railed between these emotions constantly and continuously: absolute awe for what is, and then the deep anguish of fear, wearing yourself out, exhausting yourself with the anxiety of not knowing the outcome of your disease, and of not knowing the steps ahead.

You wanted a definitive understanding of your disease as if this information would change things. This is like the clients you have, who only want to know what is in the future; they want to get past the present, not looking into what is. You yourself were like this for many years, before your consciousness began.

As if knowing the statistic for your particular aspect would solve anything, or change your emotional response.

You will notice you did not hear your surgeon give you statistics: your stage, your plotted outcome. We disallowed this information from arriving to you, in the beginning. We disallowed it several times: both he from delivering it, and you from hearing. It was only later, when you had been through the passage that we allowed you to know.

This is some of what we are able to do: not just giving signs and synchronicities, but also blocking information that will take you on wrong course, or a course that is not useful to the Divine outcome.

Yes, to Divine outcome, we say. This is very different from earth outcome. It is often perceived as miracles, but it is simply the way.

—The Messages.

CHAPTER 9

Grief

IN SOME CIRCLES, people have the idea that you attract what you think; what you believe is what will come to pass. Sometimes, this means people suppress or stuff their true feelings in order to keep their thoughts positive or upbeat. This results in saying positive affirmations in present tense language, such as:

I am healthy.

I am cancer free.

I am free from disease.

I am healed from cancer.

I am healthy and robust.

I enjoy a long lifetime.

And so forth.

I have always found that manifesting in this way, by creating a sort of false positivity, doesn't serve us. I don't believe Law of Attraction, The Secret, positive thinking, affirmations, manifesting—whatever name you want to give this line of thought—is of value to us when used in this way.

To my mind, it's more important to uncover what is in our true hearts than to fill our minds with what we do not yet believe.

For example, what I *really know* today, months after my surgeries as I am writing this book—what I *really know* to be true, is this:

In this moment, I am cancer free.

In this moment, I am alive.

The rest of it? *Will I be cancer free for life, or will I have a remission? Will I live a long time, or will I die young?* I readily admit I don't know.

Putting false positives on things, saying affirmations for what I know isn't true, as the Law of Attraction dictates, doesn't help at all. In fact, it can be damaging to tell the body lies and refuse to see what's actually there. Using affirmations in this way is a betrayal of the body.

When I had cancer, I did have cancer. Cancer was in my body; no positive affirmation could change that.

You notice I'm not speaking of miracles; positive affirmations and miracles are different things, which we'll talk about later. But in terms of reality—when I faced the fact of my own mortality, of dying much sooner than I'd ever imagined—I had to look at that possibility. Science, medicine, rational analysis showed it was real, it was true: cancer showed up in the scans. This reality made me incredibly sad.

I couldn't push the cancer away. I had to look at it, feel it, allow it—I had to stop pushing sadness away with false positivity—I had to go through sadness, surrender to it, and come to terms with it. This was an enormously difficult passage.

◆　◆　◆　◆

I cried when I woke up. I cried drinking my coffee. I cried in the shower. I cried dressing for my day. And that was just the morning crying—the afternoon and evening and night crying also continued.

Everything seemed monumentally precious to me: I'd look out the window to see Steve working in the garden, and begin to heave and wail. Dropping my daughter off to school, I would sit in the car afterwards and fall into absolute despair—not only because I might be leaving her, but that I would cause her so much pain by leaving her. It seemed unbearable that such a young, beautiful, hopeful girl—a girl who'd already gone through so much with her scoliosis surgery—might lose her mother.

I must admit, I became morbid.

I didn't think too much about my funeral, or if I'd be buried or cremated; if people would come to my funeral; if I would go to heaven or hell. I've never been interested in how my body would be disposed of upon death, and a funeral isn't a ceremony I think about.

I've long since settled my beliefs about heaven or hell—my own experience with the dimension beyond the veil assures me we do not end when we die—our souls continue eternally.

My morbidity focused on other questions: what would happen to my children? My partner? Even my stuff—I'm not a person who has a whole lot of stuff, but there are small, personal belongings I've delighted in for many years—where would these go? Who would untangle the mystery of my finances? Who would manage my writing in progress—pages and pages that had not yet seen publication?

And even worse: what would be the progression of my death? Would I lose my hair, as my father did? Would I become emaciated, like him? Would I become exhausted by the smallest efforts? Would I lose my ability to think? Would I be able to do little but sit on the sofa, unable to work or think, in a haze of pain and morphine until the end? How long would it take? How long did I have? What was the meaning of my life, anyway? What was the meaning of my death? And so on, and so on.

A stronger person would have snapped out of it. A different person wouldn't have allowed this wallowing in morbidity, but I have always been overly sensitive, overly emotional. I've always been deeply aware of our precious time here on this earth; of how fast it goes, how fleeing it is, and how everything can shift in one moment.

To try and put on a positive face at this time wasn't possible. I needed to go deep into my grief, and rock into the bosom of my pain and sadness. This was a part of my process, the second spiritual lesson I had to learn.

◆ ◆ ◆ ◆

That your life exists in a container of time—the time span that exists between your birth and death—is what makes it precious. Your earth life is precious because it is limited. Your human experience is precious because it ends. In the etheric realm, all is eternal. In the human realm, the container is what helps you to grow.

—*The Messages*

◆ ◆ ◆ ◆

I wasn't just sad because of what I'd miss in the future. I also cried and suffered greatly when I looked at all the harm I'd done to others in my lifetime. I went through yet another review of all the times I'd behaved badly, the friendships I'd lost, my divorce from my children's father. When I stacked everything up and looked at my life again, I didn't come out beautiful, or nice, or elegant. I came up horrible, flawed, and faulty.

I'd made a lot of mistakes, hurt a lot of people, caused a lot of pain. These actions could not be undone. I wasn't so much worried about my "sins" and how they'd affect my karma or my chance of getting into heaven. That's not my belief system; I don't think that way. I see myself as a whole person, and this means the good, the bad, the all of it, but now, in doing this kind of life review, I felt lousy. Rotten. That I'd been so stupid in the past … for much of my life, I'd been generally unconscious and ungrateful. I'd taken things for granted instead of being down on my knees at every spare moment, thanking the Divine for the amazement that is this life.

I wasted time. I squandered opportunities. I hurt some people. I betrayed others. I walked away when I should have stayed and stayed when I should have walked away. I'd been lazy, obstinate, and rude.

I'd been afraid when I should have been powerful, and brazen when I should have been humble. On occasion after occasion, I had not been my best self, my highest self. I'd been so much less.

This came crashing over me all at once, and the knowledge made me sad.

And the worst of it? Even after I saw so clearly all my flaws, faults, and foibles, even after I saw so clearly how often I'd behaved badly, made mistakes, treated others poorly ... I continued to do so. During the week before my surgery, I didn't just sit around feeling morbid. I was also cranky, rude, complaining, miserable, needy, demanding—the list goes on. I wasn't a paragon of Divine being-ness like I wanted to be.

I was a scared, desolate, and despairing human being.

But, to my surprise, in letting myself wallow in sadness, and in allowing myself to look at all the parts of my life I would miss when I died, and all the ways I hadn't lived as I wanted to, something changed.

The answer to my intense look at death was this: *Of course I was dying. I still am.* You are too. We are each slipping away from life from the moment we are born. This life isn't eternal. Our lives as souls are, but our human life is terminal.

And so, I traveled down that long hallway of looking at everything: my life, my relationships, the things I'd done well, the things I'd done wrong, what I still wanted, what I would miss.

I grieved it all. I let it go. I accepted that my reality might indeed be an early death.

And as these things happen, when I had thoroughly convinced myself my death was imminent, I received a vision telling me this was not so.

Part Two
Miracles

CHAPTER 10

Panic

PANIC PINNED ME BY THE THROAT and didn't let go.

I was lying underneath a large, white machine that filled an entire white, high ceilinged room. The machine covered my body, pressing down within an inch above my face. I could not move my head. I could not roll out. I could not slide out.

I could not move.

In a best-case scenario, all I could do was call out to the technologist, a young woman uninterested in wasting time raising the machine off my face every time I panicked.

"Do you have claustrophobia issues?" she asked, in a manner that made me suspect how I answered: *yes, no, I don't know,* wouldn't really matter.

I was pinned under the great white wing of a machine as smooth and sleek as a space ship, lowered so close to my body that I had no chance to get out. This wasn't an MRI or cat scan. This particular machine would map the path of dye moving through my body.

For someone else, this kind of situation might have been no big deal. The procedure didn't even hurt very much: the only pain was when the physician came in and gave me four quick needle pricks on my shoulder, in the place where the mole had been removed. This was almost painless, but for me, the sensation of being trapped, held down, forced to remain motionless, was too much to bear.

My face grew hot, my chest began to pound, and I started crying like a three year old, even as I desperately hoped someone would come and hold my hand.

The technician was not interested.

Fear came down from that ceiling, a big white horror, and sat on my chest for an hour. All of it was fear, there was no part that was not fear: the great white machine, the suffering of being trapped, and of course, the fear of the information that was arriving into the monitors even now, as the dye spread through my body, and we discovered where the cancer had spread.

♦   ♦   ♦   ♦

The reason we were using the dye, my surgeon had explained, was so we'd know where to look. Melanoma cells love to swim in the lymph system, and the place where the mole had been removed on my shoulder was close enough to my armpit and neck to make spreading a serious concern. The drainage path of the dye injected into my shoulder would show where the cancer had also traveled: armpit, neck, other armpit, groin.

The protocol was to allow the dye to travel for a certain number of minutes. After that, the drainage path was finished; whatever showed up during that time period was likely where the cancer would go.

In the best-case scenario, the dye wouldn't reach too many lymph nodes. In the worse-case scenario, it would show up elsewhere in my body. We had no way of knowing until the dye ran its course.

"Okay, I'll be back to check on you in 20 minutes."

The door clicked shut. The machine pressed down and the whirring began. Fear descended, and held.

♦   ♦   ♦   ♦

Pinned underneath, unable to turn my head or move in any way, I did not know how I could endure. So I took the only course of action available to me under the circumstances: I took myself into deep meditation and asked my guides for help.

Meditation is a process I do nearly daily; it is a part of how I work. My process is to simply close my eyes and take a few deep breaths. Normally, I will enter an altered state of consciousness, or what I call "light trance" in a matter of a few breaths. By now, my body is so accustomed to entering this zone of deep relaxation that simple breathing takes me there.

But this time I had trouble.

The room itself was not suited for mediation, prayer, or anything Divine whatsoever. Devoid of warmth, I felt no hint of soul anywhere in the room. Now, I believe the Divine is everywhere—but it was hard to find in this room. I scanned the room energetically, trying to find some living thing, or even something infused with living energy that I could ground on.

I found nothing.

This white, sterile room contained no plants, no warm fuzzies, not even a picture of nature or a travel poster I might crane my neck to focus on. The room had been divested of everything and anything human, animal, plant, living, or sacred. I was surprised to notice this: that in a hospital setting, where people need comfort more than anything, all comfort had been removed. Having music play, surely something easy for the hospital to arrange, would have helped, but there was nothing.

This was a place of disassociation and abandonment, the domain of machines.

I was left alone in the room. Behind a smoked glass window, the technician sat doing the things all people do when they're waiting for a task to be completed: drank her latte, checked her computer, worked her smart phone. I was being monitored, I assumed—but not carefully, not with concern.

I was just a dye path to be completed under protocol.
My own self had nothing to do with it.

CHAPTER 11

Only One

I CLOSED MY EYES AND BEGAN TO BREATHE: in through the nose, out through the mouth, in through the nose, out through the mouth. Soon, I began sliding into a place, a layer or level, as I call it, that I was familiar with.

This layer or level of consciousness is something people who meditate regularly will recognize—it's a way of entering into trance that can take you to a state of relaxation, bliss, nirvana.

This level can also deliver you to a place of peace, where you are very, very far from the cares and concerns of normal earth life. This is the kind of layer or level of conscious reality used by shamans who walk barefoot across a bed of coals, or gurus who survive on nothing but air for months on end.

This is not mind control, as is commonly believed.

It is mind surrender.

◆　◆　◆　◆

People who meditate understand the importance and usefulness of this deep connection to another realm of consciousness. Connecting with the Divine is like having the ability to go on a mini-vacation wherever you are, no matter what stress or chaos is going on around you. The more you practice, the more time you spend in meditative vibration, the easier it gets to go there quickly.

People who pray also understand what a great comfort it is to "enter in" and petition before God. To give thanks, to lay down your worries and burdens, to ask for assistance. I no longer belong to a formal religion, but during my time as a Catholic I found the act of prayer was always the most useful thing I could do—simply by opening my heart and calling upon God, I could lift my mood, lift myself out of despair, and discovers the courage to face what was to come.

I still pray, and I love going into this place of sacred supplication. How beautiful it is to connect with God, or whatever vision of the infinite you hold in your own mind and heart. However, in this case, under the great white wing, I was attempting neither to meditate, nor to pray.

Instead, I was attempting to go into the particular layer or level of consciousness in which I would be able to access intuitive information. Mediation is a level of consciousness far from our human awareness. Prayer is a closer level. Intuitive gathering is a layer or level somewhere nearer regular awareness: it's not about going into bliss, nor is it about giving God thanks. Instead, it's the place where I go—where anyone can go—when I desire to look into the future for information about a situation, to meet with my guides, to receive a vision, and to help understand information that's useful to me, or that I need to know.

I go into this place, this psychic sweet spot, all the time. That's how I do my work with clients. In fact, this spot is where I spend much of my working day. This is a skill I use all the time, and it should have been easy to access.

And yet even as I breathed in through the nose, out through the mouth, I had trouble blocking the whirring noises and ominous pressure of the machine above me. After what seemed a long time, something in my brain remembered how to get there— the panic halted, the flight response subdued, and I felt my body move into the first wave of deep relaxation.

I didn't like where I was. I didn't like what was happening, but I was choosing to fight fear with light—I was choosing to put my consciousness into another place, outside of panic, anxiety, and doom. I was choosing to create a direct connection to the Divine, and allow this connection to inform me and heal me.

When I was relaxed enough, I directed my mind to travel to a place where I was able to "see" the dye moving through my body. I can't logically explain how I do this; it's more of a kind of "knowing" or a sense of seeing. I sensed the dye had collected in my armpit. I checked my neck, my other armpit, and my groin. I did not sense that dye had traveled there. In truth, I sensed the dye had been, or was being actively blocked, from traveling there.

By my body?

By the Divine?

I did not know. I only had the sense that dye had collected in my right armpit, the one closest to where the mole was removed. Only a few minutes had passed, and yet I already knew the dye would not spread further through my body.

♦　♦　♦　♦

This work is hard to explain to people who don't do it themselves, or don't believe in it. It's hard to explain how I "see" with my mind's eye, or third eye, but I do. I "see" what's happening—not exactly, the way a surgeon would see it if he cut open my body and looked, or the way you'd see it under a microscope in the lab or with another medical device. I couldn't "see" what the technician saw on the monitor. Instead, I see more symbolically, more metaphorically. Sometimes I see a diagram, sometimes an object, sometimes a vision that shows me the meaning. Sometimes it's just a color, a sensation, or a feeling. In this case, I had the sensation of energy in the armpit as being clogged or congested, and then, I heard words in my head: *"only one."*

Not as a voice in the room.

Not as my own thoughts.

But as a kind of a sensing of language, a telepathy, a hearing in my mind's ear.

Only one.

Only one lymph node? I wondered in my head, as I searched for more information in my body.

I felt the presence of guides and angels arrive into the room, and this was a great comfort. I'm sure they'd been there all along, but fear has a way of blocking our ability to perceive this Divine energy, this holy presence.

Only one.

I didn't know what to think. I allowed them to ease the pressure of the machine from my body; the machine was still there, but I became more comfortable in the space available to me. I asked for celestial energy to pour into my head and to fill up my entire body. I asked for healing energy to move to the place where the mole had been, and then I sensed the energy had begun to travel, like electricity, along the drain paths.

In my mind's eye, the Divine energy raced like a current through my body; very soon, my entire lymph system and several other systems were coursing with Divine energy. I noticed no dye in the groin, none in the left armpit, none in the neck.

I saw some dye, blue in my mind, in my right armpit. I looked into it. The feeling was one of congestion, of stickiness, of sluggishness. That wasn't good. But I noticed it wasn't traveling. The dye was clustering in that area only, and I had the idea that drainage would go no further.

Only one.

One armpit. That's what they meant by *only one*, I thought. But the guides became agitated at this thought; not angry, as they are never angry, but agitated in a way that felt like buzzing in my head, as they tried to get me to pay attention better, to translate more accurately.

Not one armpit.

Only one.

◆　◆　◆　◆

I didn't know what *only one* meant. As I struggled to understand, the technician came back into the room.

"Can I have a break?" I asked.

She peered down at me, like someone fascinated by a crushed bug. "I'll have to ask."

Within a few minutes, another technician, someone more senior, came into the room.

"I'd love a break," I said, as he gazed at the monitor.

"Sure, okay," he said distractedly. "We can do that."

He pressed a button and the machine began to whir and shudder. In one glorious movement, it lifted off my face by about two feet.

Freedom! I could have easily slide off the narrow table, rolled out from beneath the machine, and run like an escapee in an action movie. I could have been out the door and racing down the long, white hallway before the technician could do anything to stop me.

But I stayed there.

"It's drained to the right armpit," he announced. "But it hasn't showed up anywhere else yet."

"That's good, right?" I asked hopefully, but they don't supply opinions or encouragement there.

"We have to wait for protocol. Twenty more minutes," he said in response, and the machine shuddered down. I was left alone again, and this time, it felt even worse. I struggled to find my way into trance, and to reconnect with my guides, but I couldn't find them, and spent these minutes trying to keep my body from squirming.

After a very long time, the technician stepped back in and viewed the monitor with distaste.

"Nothing's moved." he said. "You've been here an hour. You're supposed to be done now, but…"

I waited, breathlessly, for him to push the button and raise the machine.

"We'll do another twenty minutes," he said again. "To be sure. "

He clicked out of the room, and the scanning began again.

◆　◆　◆　◆

I allowed this new information to swirl in my mind. Surely it was good, that the dye hadn't spread further? Surely it was a good sign that we had to spend more time?

I lay there for twenty more minutes, my mind out of control with worry, until he came back in the room and stared at the machine in resignation.

"Nothing further," he said, almost as if he was disappointed by my lackluster results. "Just three in the armpit."

Three! I thought in shock.

Not *only one*.

Three.

That wasn't what I'd pictured, not what my guides had told me. I was so stunned by this information—so different from what I'd been informed by my guides—that I climbed off of the table and stumbled out of the room into the long, bright white hallway, a tunnel of light and disorientation. I made my way to the parking lot and got in the car and I couldn't start it because I was crying too hard.

Three in the armpit.

This was not good news at all.

CHAPTER 12

Biopsy

A FEW DAYS LATER, I visited my surgeon to hear the official news: yes, it was a good thing the dye hadn't spread past one armpit, hadn't shown up in the neck or groin. That made things enormously less complicated, he said. but we were still left with the armpit that lit up.

"The dye showed up in three lymph nodes," he confirmed. "We'll need to biopsy."

Having never been in this situation before, I didn't know what biopsy meant. I mistakenly thought "biopsy" meant a simple in-office procedure; the removal of a tiny bit of tissue for testing.

As he talked, I realized he meant surgery, with general anesthesia, and recovery. No small procedure at all.

This happened in early October, and my plate, so to speak, was so very full.

Mid-month, I had an event in Seattle—three days of lectures, workshops, and readings. My radio show was going strong, and I was slated to start a second show in three weeks. A final book draft was due to my publisher in a week. Yet another book would release in two weeks, and my client load was full.

Family life was also hectic: my daughter was back at school, but still recovering from her scoliosis surgery. She needed to take it easy and required help to do normal activities, like picking things up, bending, lifting, and so on. She tired quickly and needed a lot of care. Most days, she still took pain medications.

My son, then 17, had a frantic schedule but no driver's license, and thus needed to be driven everywhere, all the time. My oldest daughter had just come home from a semester in Uruguay and was dealing with the culture shock of returning to college back in California. My mom was better, but still weak. Her muscles had lost condition, making it hard for her to do daily tasks or get around.

"Can I still do the Seattle trip?" I asked my surgeon, and he thought about it for a moment before replying. Time was of essence for the surgery ... but how much time?

In the parking lot, which was beginning to look all too familiar, I sat in the car and entered my surgery date into my phone calendar: October 26. I then called my executive producer at my new radio show, and after some discussion, we decided to go forward with my start date as planned—October 31.

"I'll have a week to recover," I said to her brightly. "I'm sure I'll be fine."

I drove home and this time I didn't let the fear pull me back. I let it propel me, and propel me it did. I put my head down, cleared my schedule, and slammed through all the work piled on my plate, determined to have every last bit of it done before October 26.

♦ ♦ ♦ ♦

I love working; it's always been a solace for me—the one lovely place I can retreat to where everything always makes sense. In the next weeks I wrote, taught, and took care of details, all from my home office looking out over a great canopy of trees: maple and fir for the most part, but also madrona, and even some ancient yew.

October was cool and dry, and the leaves were still falling, and it seemed every afternoon during those weeks I waited for surgery that the geese flew overhead with their honking cries, calling to me to notice the season's change. I worked and worked and worked some more, and when I was done I went outside and raised my face to the new fall sky, scanning for the geese overhead, hoping I would be allowed to live.

What made me most afraid wasn't the surgery itself: I wasn't worried about anesthesia, the surgery was simple, and I didn't anticipate any difficulty there. What most disturbed me was the discrepancy between what the results said (three lymph nodes) and what my guides had told me.

Only one.

♦　.♦　　♦　　♦

Over the past four years, I've made all the decisions in my life using intuition. I've learned to trust this method of information-gathering far more than anything that rational thought has every offered me. I knew my belief system wasn't accepted in the mainstream, but that no longer bothered me. I was going to use what I knew worked, and my surgeon would use what he knew worked, and this co-joining of efforts would create a synergy of intention. I knew this; I had no doubts about it.

But why then, when my intuition had always been so accurate in the past, was it not working now?

I'd learned to trust my guides. I relied on them for every decision. Some might say this is silly, childish, brazen, magical thinking, but I'd used this system for a decade and it had never failed me.

Why now, this discrepancy?

Three on the monitor; but *only one* from the guides.

Fear seeped into my heart.

If I couldn't trust in my guides, my angels, the Divine … there was no point to the world as I knew it, the world I'd come to believe in. The darkness began to descend, as my mind eroded in panic. I had cancer, my surgery was upcoming, and my guides were nowhere to be found.

◆   ◆   ◆   ◆

We were there, of course. You know this now. You allowed yourself to spiral into a place where it was difficult for you to enter the layers and levels of consciousness where we are so readily found. Your mind spiraled, your mind panicked, and because of this energetic imbalance you could not reach us and then you panicked more.

Your mistrust in the information you received; this was a dark night of the soul for you. You have been following in Divine flow for so long, it is true. This has been a change you have accepted, and are teaching to others, but your mistrust in this one particular bit of information was a lesson for you to learn.

Not your fear of mortality; this was also so.

But fear that the entire world you understood, a world that is not readily accepted or acknowledged by most people you know, that this world was not correct. That it was you who had been duped, or you who were living in fantasy.

You know now, this was incorrect. You know we are real and available to you, as real as anything in your life. In fact, we are more available to you, because we exist always with you, in all lifetimes.

It is a difficult path; this path of Divine understanding, when the world is based on earth understanding. The mystic, the healer, the intuitive, the elemental, the yogi, the healer. All these are names for those who understand. These are real; this is the real work. And yet these are still thought of as incorrect, dangerous, and subversive.

You know now: rationality is just one perspective. There are many ways the Universe works. Miracles are indeed possible, and they are in fact the true way energy moves. You have your life working in this way, and in the last decade, you have come to know this as so.

We know it was very difficult for you to turn away from us; to believe you did not see us. We let you rest at this time. We could have stomped and barraged and shouted to come into your awareness. We worked instead, with the music.

—*The Messages*

CHAPTER 13

Mantra

MUSIC IS WHAT SAVED ME from this second bout of fear, on those mornings when I woke up at 3:00 a.m. wondering how many days I would have left on this planet ... and could not sleep again. The surgery would reveal everything: whether or not the cancer had spread, where it had spread to, and how far it might have gone. The surgery was 20 days away, now 18, now 17.

Each day was like the agonizing end of a pregnancy, in which you are so ready to give birth, and yet the baby is equally unready to arrive.

Each day of waiting was like this—a chance for the fear to spiral up, defeating all possibility of hope.

◆ ◆ ◆ ◆

The possibility of my death filled my mind: but how could it be time for me to leave this world, my partner, my family, all the people I loved, my writing and teaching which had only just begun?

How was this possible?

And yet it was. These things happen every day. I was no more immune than anyone. This not knowing and this knowing began to take over my mind, until I could think of nothing else in the days before surgery.

This continued, an endless spiral of fear and anxiety and misery, until I found the music.

♦　♦　♦　♦

When I first discovered mantra it felt odd, silly, overly simplistic. This hadn't been a part of my upbringing, and in fact I'd never heard of it until I met my partner, an expert in sound healing who'd studied it for decades.

"This music is weird," I commented when I first heard it. "It's the same words over and over again."

He just smiled.

"Why aren't there any lyrics?" I complained after listening again. "Why does the melody keep repeating—it's too simple. It's boring, it's too simple, it's…"

And then of course, I couldn't say another word, as I was too busy falling into space, my body sliding down and my mind drifting off to dimensions unknown. I was so tranced out, I slumped over from my sitting position and couldn't move. I could not speak. I could not think rationally. I had astral projected to somewhere else entirely, and the angels came down and the guides emerged and I was healed, transformed, and transmuted.

After that experience, I no longer questioned the Divine power of mantra. Thus, mantra plays on a pretty regular rotation at our place: we play it on the stereo, we play with our own musical instruments and voices, and we sometimes record it, with our band Martyrs of Sound.

I don't know how I could have forgotten mantra, during all those days and weeks of fear, but when I finally remembered it, mantra saved my life.

♦　♦　♦　♦

When you began to breathe, your vibration shifted. When you began to use mantra, your entire being changed. Such is the nature of breath and mantra in the human body; such is the way music works in the universe that is your human form.

Remember this.

We say: sound heals. Sound, acts as a tuning fork for the human cellular collective: the collective that is the physical body. This is the same for your body, and for all human bodies. There is a frequency that resonates, that brings health, healing, happiness. There is a frequency that resonates, that causes disease, dis-ease and discomfort. You are able to shift your frequency by immersing yourself in the frequency you choose.

But there is more than this: mantra, which is sacred repetition, sacred repetition that inhabits the breath and the body as it is sung, allows the mind to hook into or attach to something different than the obsessive thought spiral.

And there is also more than this: music, which is as close as you can get to understanding the true nature of the Divine in your human body, allows the opening of the heart and the release of emotions. There is almost nothing else that provides this to you so quickly, except for sleep, dreaming, and the transcendence of sex.

—*The Messages.*

♦ ♦ ♦ ♦

I'd met Raghunatha Dasa earlier that summer in Ashland, Oregon at the music festival Steve and I attended. I don't remember how we met—but in the way the Universe always works when it needs to bring people together, we did. The three of us sat down on the floor of a giant yurt streaming with sunshine, and found in each other kindred souls. Life is often like this: you travel to somewhere far away, only to find a person who resonates with you as if you'd never left home.

We spoke of music, mantra, the Divine, energy, vibration and how it all comes together; to someone else this might have seemed a foreign language, but this was a language we spoke fluently, and it was a joy to speak it together.

I didn't get a chance to listen to his radio show immediately: the melanoma was discovered a week after we got back, and then everything slid out of control, but when I finally listened to his show at www.mantraradio.co, I was hooked: an hourly program of modern mantra, with Raghunatha teaching about the devotional practice of bhakti, and telling stories about ancient deities in his relaxed Birmingham-British accent.

It was raining the first day I heard his show—October bluster at its finest, but I didn't care. I put on my headphones, stepped out into the cold, Oregon gloom, and began to walk.

For an entire hour I let this music transport me to another place, as the tears streamed down my face and I strolled around our circular driveway, processing and releasing my fears, my anxieties, all my uncertainties about what was ahead—whether I would live, or whether I would die.

I started out in panic, and ended up in peace.

Thus, became my practice: sneakers, headphones, and mantra. I walked around that driveway for as long as it took: 40 times around equaled two miles, and that's usually what I did. I walked until all my tears were shed for that day, until my fears quit me, at least for that time.

CHAPTER 14

Stillness

WHAT MANTRA DOES IS TRICK THE MIND into stillness. My brain was so busy thinking about the cancer in my body and whether I would live or die, that the only way I could quiet my thoughts was by keeping my brain busy, distracted—tricked.

When I listened to mantra, the brain paid attention. Not at first—the fear spiral was locked in tight. But as the mantra worked its repetitive magic, the brain became entranced, literally entrained into a state of listening that flowed underneath all the worry and turmoil. A state of deep listening became my primary mental activity, and eventually replaced the anxiety loop. The mantra sank in, and slowly but surely became the dominant thought vibration.

I was amazed by the power of mantra to create this shift in me. From then on, I had this music at the ready; every time I noticed myself slipping into fear mode—and this might be four times in an hour—I queued up the mantra on my smart phone and essentially "rebooted" my brain.

As I saw how my mood shifted and panic quelled with just a few minutes immersion into the music, I began using music even more intensively—not just mantra, but all kinds of music—for longer periods of time, not only as an instant brain reboot, but for longer sessions of brain rebuilding.

I would lie on the floor or sofa with headphones on, listening to *Radhe's Dream*, the healing album Steve and I had created the year previously with our band Martyrs of Sound. That album, our fourth, is based on the theories of sound healing—repetitive phrasing and trance induction. The music is extraordinarily emotional, and brings out feelings you might not even know you have. When I listened to that music, a full hour immersion of one song that soared and swooped into others and into others still, I experienced catharsis.

This was a miracle, this mantra and the music and the way it changed everything. I felt so grateful to find it at this time.

♦   ♦   ♦   ♦

People have many ideas about mantra. It's a very ancient method of chant, using words with sacred meanings to create trance and altered state. The mantras I usually use are Sanskrit, but many other ways exist.

Some believe the chanted repetition of a single mantra, such as the word *Om*, is in itself a holy act; that the saying of this word is a Divine experience. What I experience is the entrainment or enchantment of the mantra's repetition into trance. This method of connecting to the Divine absolutely produces shifts in our breathing, shifts in our consciousness, shifts in our body's vibration, and shifts in our mood and attitude. I believe this creates healing at the deepest level.

♦   ♦   ♦   ♦

Mantra is the word. Music is the flow. The vessel that both are poured into is your body: the collection of cells that create the universe that is your human form. When you pour mantra and music into this vessel, everything shifts and changes, and the possibility for healing is created, time and again.

When you continue to pour this vibration, this Divine infusion into your body, you begin to heal all that is within. You reset your vibration in alignment with this higher, Divine vibration.

When your vibration shifts into highest vibration, darkness is replaced with light. The darkness is the illness, in the body or the mind. The light is the mantra and the music, which carries within it the Divine vibration you require to be lifted to Divine frequency.

Over and over during the terror of your cancer, you shifted your vibration to the highest levels of Divine, using mantra and music. This created a vibrational alignment in your self. Darkness turns toward light. The law of levity trumps gravity.

When you rise up in your spirit, your body is also lifted.

—*The Messages*

♦ ♦ ♦ ♦

Mantra also helped me find the vibrational level in which I could connect with my most familiar guide, Hajam. Some of you know about this guide, as I wrote about him in my first book *Writing the Divine*. Hajam was the first spirit guide to arrive at the start of my intuitive journey and has arrived to me continually since then.

I asked Hajam the question, "What shall I do?" about the cancer. He showed me the tambourine or drum he held in his hand, and told me to "celebrate, be joyous, relax, rejoice, and have fun!"

"But I have cancer," I wailed to him, and he would shake his tambourine at me. "This is the way to live," he told me over and over, laughing and dancing, even as I resisted. "This is how your energy should be, to create the healing you desire."

"But…"

"Be happy, be free, eliminate stress. Enjoy, experience, don't worry."

"But…"

"There is nothing else," he would tell me again and again. "Dance, sing, be."

And even though I didn't yet believe him, I began to move in that direction with my life. Instead of feeling terror and depression about my cancer and the upcoming surgery, I began to experience a kind of exultant joy in many of my waking hours. It was strange to have my world falling apart, and yet to have such experiences of joy in each day.

CHAPTER 15

My Father's Gift

WHEN MY DAD SHOWED UP during my cancer journey, he had a full head of hair.

This was significant, because at the time of his death, he was entirely bald from chemo. Yet before that, for his entire life, he'd sported at thick head of hear—it was wavy, reddish golden and never seemed to go grey. I inherited my hair from him, and my son also has his trademark hair.

Thus, my dad showing up with hair was the first signal that all was well—that I would not have to do chemo; I would not have to lose my hair, and as he became even more specific with his messages, I began to feel hope.

Nothing special happened to bring my father to me. As you've caught on by now, communicating in other realms, with other beings, is an everyday activity for me. This is something that often happens when I enter meditation or trance; it isn't a skill that's unique to me, it's just how it works.

Thus, no angel trumpets, no herald announcements: my dad just showed up when I needed him the most.

My dad has communicated with me frequently since he passed more than a decade ago. In the first few months after he died I'd see him all the time: he'd be sitting on a sofa, or standing right beside me in the room, very clear, an apparition.

Later, he came in a more shamanic style vision—he showed up as an eagle—an Amercian bald eagle—in places where eagles didn't live. For example, early one Christmas morning, I went for a walk outside my mom's house and saw an eagle in the heart of Seattle, about 20 feet up a fir tree.

"Hi Dad," I said. "Merry Christmas."

These visitations were great miracles of understanding for me, and they happened many times and in many places during the first years after his passing. As time went on, I found it harder to reach him. Thus, when he first came to me during the weeks before my surgery, I didn't expect it—I'd actually given up trying to reach him.

The visitation happened simply—I'd been crying and I was resting, lying on the sofa in the front room. My eyes were closed and I felt exhausted. Suddenly I began to sense my father and soon after I began to see him in my mind's eye, clearly, and differently than before.

In the other times he'd contacted me, he'd always shown up bald, the way he'd looked at his death, but this time, he appeared much younger: in his late 30s or early 40s, I'd guess—and again, with a full head of hair. He was also dressed differently, in something I'd never seen him wear—carpenter pants with a hammer loop on the leg, and an oversized T-shirt. This was significant, because my dad was a Brooks Brother guy, a preppy dresser, an intellectual.

In fact, our standing family joke was that the only carpentry he'd ever done was with duct tape. Yet here he was, loaded down with tools: hammers, levels, T-squares, all kinds of things you'd use for building. In his arms he held a variety of wooden slats and boards.

A small building stood behind him, which I first took to be an outhouse. I remember thinking: this is the weirdest spirit visitation

I've ever seen, featuring an outhouse! But he laughed and shook his head: it wasn't an outhouse. The building was a small shed-like doorway to an enclosed bus stop or a tiny cabin; a rough wooden structure containing a doorway to somewhere else.

Then I realized: this was a portal, and it was a portal to the other side.

♦　♦　♦　♦

In my vision, my dad was satisfied I understood this was the doorway beyond the veil. The moment I recognized this, I asked him "Am I going to die from this cancer?"

Instead of answering in telepathy, which is how I often experience communication with the departed, my dad got busy hammering boards and slats all over the door, the way you do when you're securing a building from trespassing and making sure no one can enter.

My dad hammered boards all over that doorway, and when he was done, he turned to me with a big smile and started waggling his finger at me.

"You're not allowed in here yet," he told me in my mind. "You're not coming in here yet—you're not allowed."

This made my head spin.

He laughed again, gesturing to show how much he enjoyed his new carpenter outfit. He looked fit and muscled, quite different than he had in his later years.

"It's not your time. Don't think it is." he said again.

As I sat there still in shock, he hammered even more boards over the opening, the door, the portal to death.

Then the vision faded, and I understood deeply and without doubt, that I wasn't going to die.

I didn't understand how I wasn't going to die from melanoma— that's not what the vision told me, but I understood with clarity, courtesy of my dad as a carpenter, that now was not my time.

♦　♦　♦　♦

Sara Wiseman

I had looked at sadness, I had grieved the end of my life. And now my father arrived and told me to knock it off, that I wasn't going anywhere and I'd better get used to sticking around, because that's what would happen. Now it was time to move out of fear and grief and into my next spiritual lesson: deciding to live.

CHAPTER 16

Trust

After I my father's visit—after he showed me that not only was the door to the afterlife closed to me, the gateway was actually boarded up, with a big "no trespassing" sign plastered on it—I relaxed a little.

This was exactly the confirmation I needed to understand that I wasn't going to die from cancer—it just wasn't in my Divine destiny at this particular time.

Now, it might seem difficult to understand how I could trust this vision. I'll admit that although I did trust it, I had trouble allowing myself to completely believe it.

As an intuitive, I work all day "in the field" as it's sometimes called. This means, I work in different layers or realms of consciousness. I often work in trance, looking into the past and future. I also work "beyond the veil" which means I communicate with entities that aren't human: spirit guides, angels, and the departed.

After so many years of working in the field, which is of course a field of work that is mostly undocumented, unresearched and considered non-scientific, non-medical, woo-woo and even evil, depending on who you ask, I've learned to trust.

I trust the visions I get; I trust the messages; I trust what I receive from guides and the departed. I trust implicitly, and I advise my clients and students to do the same.

Why then, did I have trouble trusting what my father showed me?

On the one hand, I completely believed his message.

On the other, everything in the real world—the world of medicine and science and even what my friends and family told me—lead me to distrust it.

And here's where the problem of fear came in.

For even as I worked to stay out of panic, fear rumbled into town like a posse of bad guys come to visit when the sheriff was away.

The dichotomy was clear: a beautiful vision from my departed father showing me all was well versus a mind that had trouble keeping out of the fear spiral.

After several more visions I finally got it. I finally understand all was well, even though I had no proof, no science, no results yet.

♦ ♦ ♦ ♦

You had said before in earlier years, that you were not afraid to die. When you met death the first time years before, you knew God in that moment, and you saw death for what it was: a glorious reunion with the Divine, yourself shifting out of the challenges, and yes, even the suffering of living in an earthly body, and you believed you were ready.

But this is only what you thought. The lesson hadn't yet been integrated. In your first near death experience, you only slipped around the edges of death's veil—the portal that would take you permanently there. Even in your work, you had only been to the portal; you had not actually gone through the portal yourself.

You only shimmied up the drainpipe, so to speak, to come to the areas where we live, where we exist, and where the departed, as you call them, are readily available to you.

This knowing, this understanding of the eternal aspects of what is beyond the veil, is not the same as picking up and leaving your earth body. It's not the same, especially, as saying good bye to all life experiences and the people you have known in this life.

Your children, for one. They are bright spots your life, soul of soul to you. You were not ready to leave them, not only because of your feeling of responsibility to them, but because of your own sense of loss, of having to be parted from these souls.

Your partner, for another. This great love of this lifetime has not found you in lifetimes previously. You are new to each other, and you recognize this; the newness that you have for each other, this sense of souls merging perhaps as the first lifetime you have been on earth, or one of just a few lifetimes.

It is true, you have not skirted around this soul many times. He is new to you, as you are to him. And with him, you are finding an entirely new level of understanding, consciousness and of love. Love in the physical, love in the emotional, love in the etheric.

All manners of love are brought to you in your association with this man, and it was heartbreaking to think that you would be taken from this lifetime and not allowed to have these experiences.

And then finally, for you, the sheer experiences that you have in your life: the times you spend thinking and writing, the times you work with others, the times you sit quietly among the trees, or watch the moon rising in the sky, or the ocean in all places. These are meaningful to you in profound ways. These are also part of your understanding of love.

We say: do not worry about your imminent death. The first death, in the first accident, the near death experience? That has past. This second death, this brushing against the veil with cancer? This is also closed to you.

There will be other experiences, but the cancer experience is closed to you now. You've learned what you needed to learn in that span of time, and you will continue to learn more in further integration

The soul ... your soul, another's soul, travels the same path: Always toward consciousness, toward more growth, toward greater understanding.

The human self ... yes, as you know, it does rage and flounder. It is full of failings, misaligned and back-stepping into the lower vibration of pain.

But this is not where you are going now.

You are not going to die at this time. Not today, not tomorrow, not soon. That particular aspect has been lifted from you. You will die, when the time is yours. But this is not now.

Thus, we ask that you get the rest you need to support your human body, as you are going to need it for some time. We have seen in you the habits of giving up, of running yourself to exhaustion, of over-work. Don't succumb to these. You will be unhappy later on that you did not become wise early, in keeping your body healthy. You will need your body later, and you will be very happy, if you have kept it in a state that provides comfort and ease. .

—*The Messages*

CHAPTER 17

Hemp

TEN DAYS BEFORE SURGERY, I was making progress. I had learned how to keep my mind out of fear, with a daily practice of meditation, mantra, and walking. Usually two miles in the wet, blustery darkness did the trick, often starting out with tears pouring down my face along with the rain, and ending up feeling something different at the end—not quite calm, but resolute.

I'd also surrendered to mortality—I'd looked at dying from melanoma, and I knew it was a distinct possibility. My surgeon hadn't given me statistics—he wouldn't even tell me my cancer stage until much later, but I did my own research, and I knew what it looked like.

It could go either way, survive or die.

After looking at death, staring down that path and seeing it as a real possibility ... I decided to resist.

That sounds easy enough—a forgone conclusion.

But if I get truly honest, I need to say ... it wasn't.

When you're in so much fear, when things are so stressful and you don't know what lies ahead, it's so easy to let yourself give way, to slip away, to allow cancer to spread and grow. In some ways, giving up was an easier option—to give way and know a certain outcome.

In some ways, the decision to live was harder—especially with that very real chance of failing.

But, even if I might not succeed ... I was determined to try, and that meant trying everything at my disposal.

◆ ◆ ◆ ◆

A friend implored me to use hemp oil, and soon afterwards I began slathering hemp oil all over my arm and my arm pit where the three lymph nodes were located deep within. The hemp oil was gritty, greenish black, and smelled like skunk.

"Don't taste it," my friend advised me. "It'll get you so high you can't function."

No problem. I wasn't interested in that.

I was interested in keeping my body and mind as clear as possible: no alcohol, drugs, or medications whatsoever. I also gave up junk food and took handfuls of vitamins every day, something I usually didn't bother with. My diet, usually good, became even more pristine and plant based. I had plenty of fresh, clean air. I got lots of sleep.

In terms of health habits, I really cleaned up my act.

When I heard about hemp oil, I didn't have much reaction. It didn't seem to resonate with me. On the other hand, with just ten days before surgery, I wanted to do everything I could to heal myself.

With hemp oil, there was no real harm if it didn't work, and if it did work? That risk was easy to take.

◆ ◆ ◆ ◆

I've always been fascinated by how the flora and fauna of this earth seem to hold every cure we need. Researchers recently discovered that bees may hold a possible solution for HIV. Sea slugs are being researched to one day produce clothing fiber. Since ancient times, humans have used medicinal plants of all kinds.

We're still the infancy of understanding how medical marijuana works—along with so much other flora and fauna. At the time of this writing, legislation has just passed to legalize marijuana in Washington and Colorado, and other states will follow.

I'm not interested in the high of marijuana—I'm in a trance for so much of my day, in meditation or working with clients, that I get enough of that state. For me, staying grounded and balanced is the reality I seek.

Many claim hemp oil is a miracle cure for melanoma. At this point, I didn't see any reason not to try it: I slapped hemp oil liberally on my arm, and washed my hands carefully afterwards.

I'd told my surgeon what I was going to do, and to his credit, he didn't scoff or berate me. I don't think he believed I could change anything using holistic techniques—from hemp oil to meditation—but to his credit, he never said so. He did keep me focused on the traditional course, which was surgery, and I accepted that, too.

We were each doing our part: he was taking care of the traditional medicine, and I took advantage of other kinds of healing—Divine, energy, holistic.

♦　♦　♦　♦

By this time, I had several clear goals I wanted to manifest before surgery.

My first goal was to stop the cancer from spreading.

My next goal was to eradicate the cancer, if possible.

I wasn't focused on my arm; I felt the cancer had already been cleared from there. I was deeply focused on my armpit, where we'd seen the dye in three lymph nodes.

When I returned from surgery, my goal was to hear the words "tissue clear."

I had no idea how to do this. But I was going to try.

CHAPTER 18

Blip

IT'S ONE THING TO BE INTUITIVE for other people. It's quite another to do it for yourself.

As I began the countdown before surgery, I knew I needed help. Even though I battled my mind back from fear and I was fierce in my intention to live, I still felt confused by the message from my guides of "only one," and why their message was inconsistent with the three lymph nodes that showed up.

I needed someone neutral to take a look; I also needed someone who spoke my language.

Debra Lynne Katz was the natural choice because she'd already been a big part of my spiritual journey. She's the author of several outstanding books on psychic development, and we've worked with each other off and on for years. When I told her about my situation, she immediately agreed to help.

I must confess: I was nervous. Debra and I have the same stance on refusing to "sugar coat" readings, and I knew she'd tell me the truth, even if it was dire.

I entered our connection with trepidation and hope.

We worked by phone. After a few minutes of chatting, we got down to business: I went into a lightly relaxed state on my end, and Debra went into a state of deep relaxation on hers. She took her time, allowing the information to reveal itself. To my great relief, her first words were exactly what I'd been hoping to hear.

"This cancer thing … it's just a blip," she said. "I know you might find it hard to believe, but it's a blip."

"A blip?"

"It's something small, something you're going through now but it won't be a big deal later … it's not a big part of your life."

Even though I was relieved at her words, I still felt concerned.

Melanoma—a blip? Perhaps Debra thought I had another, simpler form of skin cancer. Maybe that's why she didn't see the danger.

"Melanoma is a very serious cancer," I told her. "It's one of the deadliest."

"Yes," she agreed. "I understand, but this not a death sentence for you. You're not going to die from it."

I let out a long breath and the top of my head suddenly felt very light.

"The cancer's here for other reasons," she stated suddenly.

And then, "What caused the cancer?"

I expected this question, and I had several answers prepared: I'd been overworking, I was overstressed, it was some kind of Divine retribution for my divorce years before, that it all had to do with getting sunburnt in Hawaii when I was a kid, that I was a strawberry blonde and thus prone to melanoma, and my father had melanoma. But when Debra asked that question in her direct tone, something different came out.

"I think … I took on some kind of karma, for my mother. She almost died this past summer…" I paused, realizing that even though I'd never thought of this idea before, it was entirely true. "My mom was really sick, in the hospital for six weeks, and I think … I think I took it on for her."

Debra laughed, with her light silvery laugh.

"It's funny you thought you had to make yourself feel bad, in order to help someone else feel better!" she said.

I didn't laugh, but I heard her.

"I also think I took on my daughter's karma, when she had her scoliosis surgery that summer." I added. "I'm okay with that; I was happy to do it for her."

Debra didn't say anything, and I'm not sure she agreed. I needed to think that one through myself. Is it okay to take karma for one's children? As parents, is that our job—to take on our kids' pain? Or are they on their own karmic path, and we don't need to do this for them? Do we all have our own karma, ours alone to keep and deal with? Or is our responsibility different for adults than for our children?

I had a sudden flash of all the people in my life for which I'd taken on karma for.

In my intuitive work, I don't do this—I simply act as witness; I don't take things personally, but in my private life, my boundaries weren't as clean. I'd often try to fix things for people or take on their pain. Over the years, I'd willingly taken on people's "stuff" over and over again.

This is common enough, and it usually doesn't make you sick.

In this case, however, the karma for my mother was strong. She nearly died from a kidney issue, and when I took on some of that illness for her—well, I realized now, it wasn't mine to take.

And my daughter during her operation? I'm not sure if this was mine to take or not.

My error.

And now, my result.

In that moment, I gave my mother back her karma. It had always been hers, and I had no business taking it on.

I still wasn't ready to give my daughter's back—she's only a child, and I'm her mother. I decided I'd carry her burden a little longer.

In my unexpected answer to Debra, I realized that while we're here to help each other, we're not here to take on other's burdens. Some beings, such as Jesus, or Buddha or the saints, the highest elevated beings, can do this—they can actually transmute the pain without taking it on themselves.

I do not think I can or should do this. I am only who I am, a person growing into a more conscious person, slowly and with struggle. Thinking otherwise was egoistic.

Debra was talking again, and I snapped to attention. "You know," she said. "I'm seeing something specific right now. I'm seeing them picking some things out of you, out of your skin. It's your doctors, and they're picking gravel out of skin—you know, like after you've fallen and skinned your knee, and gravel gets in it? They're going to have to pick all that gravel out, and that's the surgery. They have to pick it all out."

This resonated with me. This idea of gravel in my skin—that was the cancer, the little bits of pain and hurt that needed to be removed.

"There's something else," she said, laughing. "Oh, my goodness, your immune system is so strong! I see the gravel trying to get down into your body, and your immune system, it's just fighting it back!"

"I haven't been sick in years," I agreed.

"Whatever you're doing, just keep doing it!" she directed.

"My health habits certainly aren't perfect," I said, suddenly awash with guilt over my love of Chardonnay and chocolate, certain that Debra could see every indulgence. "But I do connect with nature, and I get good sleep, and I'm loved, and I'm in contact with the Divine for several hours every day."

"Yep," she said. "It's working. I've actually never seen an immune system as fully charged as yours is right now. It will take care of any complications for you."

"Complications?"

"Yes, there might be a few things that need to happen, that you don't expect."

I told her about my father's visit, and she started laughing again.

"Why are you doing this session with me? You know you can trust him!"

"I know," I said. "It's just hard when there's all this fear."

"It's a blip," she reiterated. "They just need to pick the gravel out. You're going to be fine."

CHAPTER 19

Samurais

TWITTER IS A FUNNY THING. Millions of tweets stream through my phone every second, and I usually pay them no never mind. Millions of tweets, from millions of people I don't know and who don't know me.

Tweeting seems completely random…

Except of course, when the Universe wants to step in and help me make a connection to someone I'm supposed to know.

Like Lucy from Australia.

Or Sylvia from Germany.

Or Daisuke from Japan.

Or Wendy from North Carolina.

I love how the people I'm supposed to meet show up when I'm supposed to meet them, and that's the Universe doing what the Universe does best, making connections to push you along on your path.

Wendy is an energy healer. We connected on Twitter when she asked me to be a guest on her radio show. A few days before the surgery, we also did a healing session. As we connected on the phone, she asked me to close my eyes and concentrate on my breathing. I must say, I didn't have too many expectations. I'd never worked with Wendy before, so I tried to stay open to whatever happened.

And what happened was huge.

♦   ♦   ♦   ♦

"Go into your body," Wendy said, "and notice what is there."

Immediately, I was shown a vision. "My arm is like a meadow of spring flowers," I said. "They're bobbing and waving their heads, and they're ... they're talking to me."

I breathed slowly and deeply, fully in trance, watching the scene in my mind's eye. "They're saying everything is fine—they're sort of singing it to me, in little flower voices. They're saying my arm is clear already. It doesn't need the surgery. Even though the doctors think they need to do it for protocol, the arm is already okay."

I waited for more.

"The flowers—the cells of my arm—are telling me, 'tissue clear.' They have sweet little voices, like a chorus. They say this is what is true now, and these are the words I will hear after the surgery: 'tissue clear.'"

Calmly, Wendy asked me to notice what else was going on in my body. My attention immediately shifted from my arm, to under my arm. Here, the story was quite different.

Instead of noticing a field of flowers, I was transported into a scene from ancient Japan—these visions sound almost silly to recount, but I've done this work long enough to trust what is revealed, no matter how odd it seems.

In this vision, I stood in the middle of a battlefield, and warriors—I identified them as samurais—were desperately fighting with swords and giant sticks. Fire burned all around—the whole field seemed to be burning and smoking, and I heard shouts and cries of anguish.

"It's a horrible scene," I told Wendy. "The samurais are fighting to the death." I paused to see and hear more.

"We will never let you down," the samurais shouted to me, in Japanese or whatever the language they spoke. "We will always fight for you; we will never quit."

I understood suddenly that my body was showing me, or the Universe was showing me symbolically, what was happening inside my body. I was in a battle, and in this case, the cells under my arm were fighting against the spread of the marauding cancer.

These were my samurais.

I understood then, in a flash of knowing, that my cells were putting up an enormous defense in the area under my arm, and I understood they were in an active fight to contain the disease, to keep it from spreading.

"What else do you see?" Wendy asked.

I suddenly noticed my dad was there, and he had something more to say to me.

I looked to see if he was wearing his carpenter outfit, but he was not. He was dressed casually in a kind of polo shirt and chinos. He looked young, relaxed. I waited to see what he had to tell me.

"My dad is here ... and he's showing me ... a clamshell? No. An oyster? It's open. Inside is a pearl. And he is saying ... 'pearl of great price.'"

I paused, allowing the message to come fully to me. "'Pearl of great price,' is what he's saying, but I don't understand what that means. It's something about, the cancer being condensed into one pearl, one pearl under my arm. One pearl, and the price is..."

I did not know.

The view switched and the samurais were back again, jubilantly shouting to me, "We will never stop fighting!" I was heartened by their bravery and valor.

Then the view switched again to my father, showing me the pearl. I couldn't figure it out, so I just waited, and soon various images flooded my mind: diving for pearls in the ocean, the pearls we'd seen when we lived in Hawaii when I was young, entire tanks full of oysters, in which you must choose your oyster and hope a pearl lies within it.

"Pearl of great price," my father said to me again, calmly and comfortably, holding his hands open to help me understand.

But I still did not understand what he meant. Patiently, he once again showed me the scene with the hammer—him hammering boards up on death's door.

"No" he said simply, pointing to it once again. "That's not for you."

At this point the vision began to fade: the samurais were no longer in view, I no longer sensed my father's presence. "I think that's it," I said to Wendy.

It's hard to imagine that so much can happen in the space of less than an hour: the samurais, my father's messages about the pearl—but this is what happens when you work in the realms of the Divine.

Wendy does this work, Debra does this; I do it also. There are many others in the world who do this kind of healing. This work is real, even if we don't fully understand it.

I hung up from Wendy, filled with gratitude and courage. My surgery was just seven days away.

CHAPTER 20

Carrots

By now, a few days before surgery, I'd been provided with more Divine guidance than I could assimilate.

If I'd seen this information for a client, I'd be one hundred percent clear on the outcome—I would tell my client she wouldn't die, but some work still needed to be done on the cancer. Even now it seems obvious.

But at the time, in my emotional state, I was still unsure.

♦   ♦   ♦   ♦

To a mainstream person, all the above messaging and visions might seem ridiculous—at best magical thinking, at worst delusional. Let's just say, I'm used to having my work being perceived that way. Working as I do in the field of spiritual intuition, and seeing the results time after time, I've learned to trust the visions and messaging that comes from the Divine.

So why was I having so much trouble trusting this time?

For one thing, I still didn't understand what was meant by "only one"—and this concerned me. It was a key piece of information that didn't match up—why the guides had told me "only one" when the scan and my surgeon reported three lymph nodes were in question? This didn't make sense. I didn't get it.

On the other hand, I trusted my dad's message that I was not allowed to enter death's door. I trusted the tissue on my arm would be clear—like a field of flowers. With the vision of the samurais, and seeing how intensely they were struggling, I knew the battle of metastasis was far from over.

I also understood this battle was something I could participate in, and that time was of essence. I began searching for a last ditch way to stop the metastasis.

And thus, I was delivered the miracle of the carrots.

◆ ◆ ◆ ◆

I want to clarify this statement.

First, I don't know much about plant properties, or how to use them on the skin.

Second, I don't advise anyone to use carrots in lieu of traditional or non-traditional treatments.

Third, I have no idea if the carrots I used even worked, chemically or biologically, or in any way.

All I know is that the carrots afforded me yet another spiritual experience I hadn't expected. In essence, in the process of using the carrots, another miracle was created.

◆ ◆ ◆ ◆

Edgar Cayce, an American psychic who lived from 1877 to 1945, taught about intuition and spiritual healings his whole life. One of the interesting remedies he recommended was using a castor oil poultice to draw an infection or illness out.

I'd been slathering hemp oil on my shoulder and armpit for days now, rubbing in the gritty, green-black oil that smelled like skunk. My arm was perpetually stained a horrid shade of greenish yellow, as if the whole area was bruised.

Although I wanted to believe the testimonials on how hemp oil was a miracle cure for melanoma, it didn't seem to be doing anything for me. Maybe it was, maybe it wasn't. But I didn't feel that was the solution.

I considered the castor oil, Edgar Cayce's cure, but that didn't seem to fit either. The oil seemed too strong, as it if might backfire and actually do harm to my body. Of course, these are not scientific statements; I am not qualified to have medical opinions. I'm discussing how I intuitively felt when I looked at what happened as I used hemp oil and when I considered using castor oil as a poultice.

They just didn't seem right.

I began searching for something else. To my great surprise, what resonated most was an old homesteader recipe for root poultice. This could be made with turnips, potatoes, or any root—even the common carrot. The idea was to put it on the afflicted area, and then it would heat slightly and draw out impurities.

That sounds ridiculous, right? How could carrots heal cancer?

It was a long shot—and probably crazy.

But it was also one of those days when I was basically willing to try anything. I decided to make a carrot plaster.

CHAPTER 21

Encapsulation

CARROTS SEEM SUCH SHY, gentle beings: hunkering in the ground hiding their orange faces deep in the dark earth, until one day they're plucked into light. And yet the true nature of the carrot isn't shy at all—it's heady, sweet and fragrant, with lots of juicy water stored in the root.

In fact, as I grated carrots into the bowl, I was surprised to see how much water sweated out, as if each carrot held many times its actual volume in water.

Was the carrots' ability to hold so much liquid a clue? Perhaps the drawing properties came from this ability; perhaps it worked by a kind of osmosis.

Making the plaster pleased me. It was a relaxing task, aromatic, and fun, and I enjoyed wrapping the bright reddish orange gratings into a clean, white cheesecloth. I wasn't surprised when the cloth immediately became damp and began to stain through. I got a towel to protect from staining, then lay down on the bed, raised my arm so my armpit was exposed and arranged the carrot poultice to cover the entire area.

Then I waited for something to happen.

Nothing happened for five minutes, ten, as I lay there, a little embarrassed, trying to let my anxiety go. At the worst, I'd have taken a nap with carrot on my arm, and I've certainly done dumber things in my life! But suddenly, I noticed the poultice growing warm. Sure enough, my underarm began to tingle, and I felt a pulling sensation from deep within my arm pit—almost as if the poultice was drawing impurities to the surface.

Was this my imagination? I don't know.

At this point, something shifted in me—perhaps the ridiculousness of the situation, the desperation of me slapping carrots under my arm to fight cancer—I suddenly didn't care any more. I let go of the need to know if the carrot poultice was or wasn't working.

I simply allowed it to be what it was. I closed my eyes and focused on the area under my arm. And this … this moment of surrender to not knowing, to not controlling, was when the miracle occurred.

As I placed my attention on the skin under my arm, I began to sense the cells there, as I had before in the healing with Wendy. Once again, I saw the samurais, valiantly fighting. Once again there were fires, but this time they were contained—they were small, damped down, like fires in a camp that's just broken, and there was a sense that the enemy would soon arrive.

And yet, even as defeat seemed eminent, the samurais began to shout to me with more vigor. "We will hold the line," they shouted, their voices hoarse. "You can depend on us."

I went deeper into trance and my armpit started to tingle—it tingled so much it felt like it was almost burning. It felt like … well, if you ever read *James and the Giant Peach* as a kid, and come to the spot where James as a young boy drops the magic crystals on the ground and they immediately sink into the earth, all their sparkly green dissolving into the earth, that's what happened to my armpit.

Something was sinking in—whether it was carrot, or energy, or light, I have no idea. Suddenly, the tingling took hold, and I felt the pain, the foreign bits, the cancer—that all of these were suddenly clumping or coalescing or coagulating under the pit of my arm. The area had activated, it was on fire, but without heat.

Even as I experienced this, there was suddenly more: a fleet of guides—tall ones, pale and covered in robes of light—came into my awareness. I have seen these guides many times in my work with clients; they're a sort of a medical team, a type of Divine surgery group who create healing. I have held space for this process so my times for others, but this time they came for me.

The guides began to work under my arm, picking out grit in some areas where there was more density. They removed probably 20 of these little specs of grit. I remembered, as they were doing this, how Debra had talked about the gravel; the gravel under the skin, and how it needed to come out.

I find it hard to explain how the guides did this work. It's as if they were hovering beside me, using a kind of precise instrumentation, such as long tweezers. The process didn't hurt; in fact, I couldn't feel anything. I just had the clear knowing that these things, these pieces of cancer—these pieces of grit—were being removed.

I was in deep trance as the guides worked on me, and I began to experience a kind of gathering or clustering sensation—as if the the cancer under my arm was clustering into one spot. I don't know how long I was in this state, and eventually I fell asleep.

♦ ♦ ♦ ♦

When I awoke, I felt deeply rested and at peace.

I scanned the energy under my arm and immediately noticed it felt completely different. Instead of the scattering of grey, the spreading cancer I had once sensed, I now sensed only a single spec of cancer, and I understood somehow that the metastasis had been contained, encapsulated by the work of the guides.

I understood that for now it was unable to spread any further, and it would stay this way—encapsulated, contained—until the surgery.

I knew intuitively and with certainty that my cancer had been condensed and encapsulated into a single spec under my arm, and I remembered my father's message of "pearl of great price."

Now I knew what the pearl was.

The price wasn't yet clear.

Part Three

Surgery

CHAPTER 22

Going Under

There are many in your culture who use medicine without understanding what it truly is. In expanded view, for example, surgery is barbaric. It is an absolute violation of the physical container—a practice that will seem outdated and horrific in as little as decades to come.

It is barbaric, it is violation, in the same way that cutting a limb off a tree is a violation of the tree. It's not just the cutting into the flesh and breaking the barrier of skin, either. We say: surgery in your time also means cutting away of the flesh, a permanent removal of a portion of the body.

We understand this is the modality you have available to you. But this does not disallow what the procedure is. To cut into the body, to cut away the body: you will understand later, as a people, how incorrect and how backwards this methodology is.

We also ask that you understand that surgery introduces a foreign vibration into the body—foreign objects literally go inside the body's container. Technology does not have *the same resonance or energetic vibration of the body; this creates dissonance, this creates rejection in the tissues, it takes the body a very long time to recover from this intrusion..*

Finally: anesthesia is more than a drug reaction. During the time that you exist in state of anesthesia, you exist in a twilight state. Your physicians contend that when the anesthesia takes hold, the brain gears down into an extremely low level of functioning—that you can't process or think or remember anything that happens during this time.

This is not true.

Another part of your self is fully awake at this: your Divine self. Thus, all that happens during an operation is perceived by the soul. This as real as anything you can understand.

—*The Messages*

♦ ♦ ♦ ♦

I'm swaddled up the same way I once swaddled my children when they were newborns: tightly wrapped in soft flannel, a thin blanketing that feels both light and insulating.

It's 7 a.m., and I'm eyes wide open, hyper-alert even without my normal cup of coffee. The blanketing is here to create a warm cocoon of security, and this bed-and-blanketing technique is one the hospital will use again and again. But it's a false security— it doesn't change the true reality of where I am, and what will soon happen.

I've been divested of my clothing and my glasses; identification bands have been attached to my wrist. I've stated my name and birthday and *raison d'etre*—my reason for being here, at least three times to three different people. My insurance card has been accessed like a charge card on a spending spree.

We're in pre-op, and it's nearly go time.

♦ ♦ ♦ ♦

When I first started writing this book, I was embarrassed because my cancer didn't involve chemotherapy or radiation. I didn't get sick. My hair didn't fall out. I didn't lose weight or swell up or have any side effects from treatment. How could I write a book about cancer if I hadn't gone through these treatments? How could I talk about my experience, if I hadn't had this suffering?

Finally, I figured it out.

I didn't get to skip chemo or radiation because I was lucky.

I wasn't offered them because they don't work well for the kind of melanoma I have. In others words, they weren't even options.

I was pinning it all on the surgery. There wasn't much else to do.

◆　◆　◆　◆

Steve's here with me, holding my hand and leaning over to hold me when I start to cry, which is every few minutes. So much for putting a brave face on it. I'm an emotional mess, and that's just where I am right now. The tears are streaming down, and I'm no longer bothering to stop them.

The interesting thing about Steve is that the more the pressure heats up, the calmer he gets. This morning, as I morph from person wearing regular clothing to person bundled up in hospital blankets like a baby, lying prone on a hospital bed with curtains closed around me, he gets steadier and steadier and steadier, until he's a rock—a mountain—beside me.

My gratitude for this makes me cry even more.

A woman comes in to insert needles into my hand; my IV shunt. It doesn't hurt much, but I don't like it. Even as she tapes the needles firmly onto the top of my hand, I resist the urge to pull away and rip everything off. I'm a child having a tantrum, barely being controlled by the part of me that remains adult.

The IV starts to drip and suddenly, I have to pee. I climb with difficulty out of my warm nest and wander into the hall with my gown hanging open and my metal pole wavering and manage to use the bathroom without downing the IV stand or damaging the tubes coming out of my hand. I clamber into bed again, and I'm shaking with cold.

I'm not brave at all.

Then my hand begins to pucker and sting, and I go into full-blown panic.

We are suddenly saved by a nurse who breezes in with the thickest Scottish brogue I've every heard. It is as if a Scottish version of Mary Poppins has pulled the curtains apart and entered into this tiny room.

"There, there love," she says briskly, adjusting the tape on my hand. "I've fixed that for you now. Just had a bit of pulling on the skin. You'll be fine now."

Her hands are so warm, her voice so comforting that I burst into tears yet again and she reaches over and rubs my shoulder. "There you go love," she says again. "You'll be just fine."

My surgeon arrives next, upbeat and fresh faced in green scrubs. "You ready?" he asks forcefully, as if we're about to go play a basketball championship and I'm the starting center.

"Yep," I say, and to my surprise, my voice comes out clear and strong.

The anesthesiologist swans in seconds later; a woman. She looks at me directly and takes me all in, and I immediately have faith.

In quick succession, I've met three people I know I can count on: the nurse, the surgeon, and the anesthesiologist. The fourth person I can count on is Steve, who's sitting so close he's practically on the bed.

The fifth person I can count on is me.

The sixth, seventh, and eight people I can count on aren't even human. They arrived suddenly, filling the room with their distinct and definitive presences: my father, and an entire roomful of entities and helpers and guides and angels, all here to support me.

I realize there is no time left, and I kiss Steve and say, "I love you." I start to feel woozy, and then a bit more so, and then suddenly I'm being wheeled from the curtained room, and my head explodes into ecstasy, bliss, nirvana and I feel like I'm seeing heaven.

"I haven't felt this good…" I am trying to sit up to tell this to the anesthesiologist, and I'm pretty sure I'm shouting… "I haven't felt this good … ever!"

Someone laughs.

I feel joy in every cell.

And then I'm pushed through the swinging doors into the operating room, and my surgery begins.

CHAPTER 23

The Tissue is Clear

I'M SOMEWHERE ELSE ENTIRELY while my arm is cut into and a great slice of tissue is removed. On the monitor, my brain appears to be shut down, but my soul, floating above the table, watches everything.

To disassociate now would be easy; it would be simple to die—it would be the easiest thing to have my soul leave my body now. I'm already very far away, but that isn't my path. From far away, I hear a voice booming: "Three lymph nodes taken."

It's my surgeon. I'm still swimming up from anesthesia, but I hear him. "The tissue is clear," he announces, even louder.

Another male voice chimes in, to make sure I understand: "That's a good thing!"

Yes, this is a good thing. I sink back into the drugs and the stupor with the words "the tissue is clear" resounding in my brain.

I remember nothing after that.

◆ ◆ ◆ ◆

My eyes blink open. I'm no longer in a hospital bed, but lying on a recliner. Pillows are stacked under my arm, and my arm hurts and my throat burns—which is common after having a breathing tube down your throat. All my body knows is that it's in pain. Steve is there, along with a nurse. I swoon in and out.

Then, at some point, when I'm starting to feel pain again, but before the nurse is willing to give me any more medication, I'm handed a big plastic bag of my street clothes, the curtains are rolled across , and I'm told to get dressed.

Getting dressed with only one arm working isn't easy. I pull my jeans up over my hips, and finally get them zipped. I drag my shirt on, and then place my shoes on my feet. I try by myself for a while, and then with tears leaking from my face, I drag the curtain open and ask Steve if he'll tie my sneakers.

This moment is humiliating, and scary. What else will I not be able to do? What has happened to me? What on earth has gone wrong with my arm?

◆　◆　◆　◆

An attendant wheels me out to the car, and the sight of Steve waiting there to drive me home brings on more tears. I feel relieved, happy, free, sad, and tired—a giant mix of conflicting emotions. In fact, I feel I've lost the ability to name my emotions.

The sun is bright as we drive from the city onto the country roads that take us home. Rainwater glistens on the pavement, and I notice that the trees are dripping with this crystalline wetness.

I turn my face to the window, which is the most I can do at that moment. I can't think. I can't feel. All I can do is notice this clear, bright glistening.

CHAPTER 24

Drugs

OXYCODONE IS ONE OF THE most regulated prescription painkillers in the country. To obtain these pills from a pharmacy, you need a prescription printed on special numbered form.

I was prescribed Oxycodone and took the pills for two days after I got home. I don't know if it took away the pain—I was too busy sleeping to know. After that, I went cold turkey.

Now, let me assure you, I was in pain. My arm felt like raw hamburger under the skin. I had nerve damage from my elbow, to my arm pit, to halfway down my side, and everything felt swollen, congested, thick and numb. I had no way of knowing if this condition was temporary or permanent, but it was debilitating.

Dressing, bathing, and the simplest household tasks seemed like huge obstacles. Thankfully, Steve and the kids took up most of the slack, but when it came to school transport, there was not one else to drive—and this proved to be a challenge. It's about 20 miles each way along treacherous, twisting country roads.

By the end of the morning school run my arm would be throbbing and swollen, and my suction bottle filled with blood and fluid. I'd drag myself into the house, stack pillows under my arm, and huddle under a blanket until the second driving session later afternoon.

I wasn't brave; I complained and cried and suffered.

In this way, I began to understand for the first time how people with chronic pain and illness feel. I also began to understand that any drug strong enough to knock out physical pain must also knock out the mind. And when you're in a state like this, you need your mind more than ever.

♦ ♦ ♦ ♦

I needed my mind for lots of things; but most importantly so I could meditate and reach the Divine—a source of true solace for me. I also had a practical reason for needing a clear head: in just three days my new radio show was scheduled to debut. Before the surgery, I'd talked about pushing the start date back with my executive producer, but the plans had been in place for months.

"How hard can it be?" I'd said to her so brazenly a few weeks before, when we made the decision to proceed. After all, I wasn't a newbie to radio: this would be my second year hosting my own show. Surely, starting a new show less than six days post-surgery wouldn't be that hard.

Let's just say I was wrong.

I completely underestimated my pain, my fuzzy brain, and my inability to put one word after another. But the show went on. And so, on Halloween night, five days post surgery, I drank two cups of coffee, reviewed my notes, put on my headphones … and went live.

My show has a call-in format. That means I don't have guests—it's just me, and whoever calls in from all over the U.S. and sometimes the world, to share their experiences with intuition, spirituality, and their own lives. Of course, I had support—my producer was on hand to run everything and give me my cues.

All I needed to do was watch the clock, make sure I hit my intros and outros, and then do what I always do on air, which is basically talk to people and be myself. Not too hard, right?

I made it through the first show, but looking back, I can't remember a thing about it. Two days later, I did another show, and then the schedule proceeded like clockwork: two live shows every week, as I grappled to clear my mind.

In this way, I began to understand that pain is not just suffering in the body. Pain also affects the mind, and the mind is the one thing we can least afford to be without when we are under stress, because it controls our ability to connect with the Divine.

Just when we need them most, we are least able to reach our guides and angels—those who support us without fail. When we most require solace, our minds lose ability to take us there—it's harder to find the channel, the frequency, the sweet spot. Of connection.

Thus, I found that if I took drugs for pain, my mind became too hazy to think practically or spiritually, but if I didn't take drugs, the pain took over and that in itself created a level of discomfort of distraction that made it difficult for me to meditate, pray or "enter in" as I usually do.

And in this way, I entered a dark space indeed.

CHAPTER 25

Micro-metastasis

I'M IN MY SURGEON'S OFFICE again, seven days post op, and we're reviewing what happened. My arm feels like a giant meatball—raw, swollen, and packed together.

He goes over it for me, slowly and clearly, so I can take it all in.

"The tissue is clear," the words he said to me during surgery, referred to the skin on my arm where the original melanoma had been. That tissue *is* clear, he reports; there's no more cancer there.

This is excellent news.

"Three lymph nodes taken" refers to the three lymph nodes we'd seen earlier under the nuclear scan that also lit up during surgery. When my surgeon removed them, the initial test at the time of the surgery was clear, but there's another test that's more intensive, he tells me now.

I don't faint, but almost: my head swoons, and I feel adrenaline shoot out all over my thighs. In this intensive pathology, he explains, the tissue is chopped and sliced and smeared at the smallest level. This allows the technicians to turn over every bit and examine it under a microscope.

This test is not clear.

Micro-metastasis, my surgeon explained. And then he takes a ruler from his desk drawer and shows me just how small this spec of cancer is.

Point three millimeters.

Not three millimeters.

Point three.

I stare at the incredibly small marking on the ruler, and I don't know what to say.

There's the "only one," my guides had told me about.

Only one.

And suddenly, it hits me. There's my pearl, right there—my cancer condensed into one tiny, precious micro spot. This is exactly as my guides have been telling me; exactly as I've seen in my meditations—and exactly as intuited. Shown to me now in tangible, scientific, medical reality … the *only one, the pearl* is this single micro-metastasis … a cluster of cancer *that has already been removed.*

There is no more cancer to get.

The cancer has been taken out with the surgery.

I feel so excited, so sure, I think I might be sick.

Only one. The pearl. My intuitive information confirmed finally! Already removed from my body!

Even though my surgeon is still concerned, I can't concentrate on what he's saying; I understand so clearly that it's all over—I'm cancer free. The one single micro-metastasis that needed to be caught, stopped—has been removed, and my cancer is done!

There's only one thing left that still confuses me … *only one, the pearl?* These I understand.

But my price?

Even now, I still don't know the price.

CHAPTER 26

Sacrifice

"There are a few options," my surgeon said. "One of them is do nothing."

From the tone of his voice and the way he tensed his shoulders, I knew he didn't care for that solution. He was slow in saying what came next, and he looked me directly in the eye, as he always did.

"Or you could have a second surgery."

And I knew instantly, before he said anything further that this was the last piece of my puzzle. Sitting there in my surgeon's office, as he talked through what a second surgery would entail, how we'd removed all the lymph nodes under one arm this time, not just biopsy three, how it was a bigger surgery, and there could be complications such as nerve damage and permanent lymphedema, and how it might lead to us finding out there was more cancer in the lymph nodes...

"It's the only way you'll know for sure."

He talked, I listened, and in the deepest part of my heart, my soul—wherever the place where all intuition resides, I knew I didn't require a second surgery.

I was clean. There was no more cancer to get; the tiny micro metastis, *my only one, my pearl,* had already been removed.

And yet at the same time, I knew I would go forward.

The last piece of the puzzle slid into place, and I finally knew my price.

♦   ♦   ♦   ♦

Every person has their price. On the one side of my tally were:

♦ My 13-year old daughter, who was just recovering from scoliosis surgery, plus my two other children and stepson.

♦ My partner, Steve.

♦ The rest of my family: my mom and brother, and my friends.

♦ My clients, whom I loved.

♦ My work, which was extraordinarily satisfying to me.

♦ My self, which simply wanted to go on experiencing more of this marvelous thing we called life.

On the other side of my tally was:

♦ My arm

"It's peace of mind," my surgeon was saying. "So you can know for sure."

I sat very still, taking it all in: the sacrifice of my arm for my life. My price.

CHAPTER 27

Oncologist

THE ONCOLOGIST'S OFFICE was booming, bursting to the seams with people who were really, really sick. Some used walkers; others arrived in wheelchairs, with or without oxygen tanks attached to the backs; many were gaunt, or bald, or their skin had turned to that particular shade of grey cancer brings.

This was what I expected to see.

My own appearance contrasted greatly with most in the waiting room: my hair was thick and glossy, my skin was rosy, my body round and strong. I had stamina and strength. In fact, compared to most of the people there, I was a poster child for superb health.

At first I was embarrassed—why should I look so healthy, when others didn't? Why did my cancer seem so simple, when others had to undergo the agonies of chemo, radiation and other treatment?

Steve took my hand then, and I felt his own emotional reaction to the people in the room and I realized my line of reasoning was not correct.

My situation was not simple. My apparent robust health might last—or it might not. I was at the oncologist, because a micro-metastasis of cancer had been discovered in the lymph node of my right arm pit.

I was here to discuss a second surgery, and what other treatments I might need. From a medical point of view, there was nothing simple or safe about my situation at all.

I looked at the other people waiting—the lady in the pink track suit, the man with the oxygen tank, the woman in the turban. As I looked, I began to notice something I hadn't seen before.

These people didn't just look really, really sick. They also looked happy.

The woman in the turban smiled at me broadly. The man with the oxygen nodded. Two receptionists welcomed a patient—both ran out from behind the counter and started hugging the gaunt man. Another woman, obviously in tremendous pain, graciously allowed a nurse to support her to a treatment room.

As I looked around the room, my sadness at being here—at having to go to an oncologist, and wait in a room with sick people and identify myself as sick, soon gave way to something else—something that surprised me.

The awareness that the people waiting in this room were highly conscious.

Each of them was, at some level or another, in the process of coming to terms with their cancer—with their mortality—just as I was coming to terms with mine.

We were all in the thick of it—the real, down deep stuff: the stuff we've been working on since we were kids: the hurts, the wounds, the flaws, the faults, the karma, the soul lessons we've been put here to learn.

Every person in this room was riding on the emotional roller coaster that is cancer, working their way through the lessons cancer teaches: how to keep your mind out of fear, how to face your own mortality, how to choose life, and how to choose to live in joy and love, regardless of outcome.

Some folks in this room would survive—and they'd be forever changed by their journey. Others would die from cancer—and yet that did not stop them from choosing to love and connect with those around them during the time they had left.

In the midst of the most difficult personal challenge of all, so many of the people in this room were laughing, smiling, hugging, and inviting me to join in, to come to the party and participate in their bliss. This room was like a kind of heaven on earth, but filled with sick people, instead of angels or guides.

My eyes widened as I looked around and took this all in, and then my heart got even bigger. My mouth curled up and, like a crazy person, I started smiling at everyone, and I just rose right on up into this vibration of love and connection, and I felt so grateful and privileged to be with them.

To be one of them.

♦ ♦ ♦ ♦

I liked my oncologist right away. He was a tall man with a shaved head and droll expression and, like my surgeon, he was younger than me. For some reason, I found this utterly amusing. He knew my case well, and with my surgeon had taken it before the hospital boards or round tables, where it had been extensively discussed.

He started to launch into what I could tell was going to be a complicated, technical explanation of my situation, but before he could get too far, I stopped him.

"I'm gonna do it."

He smiled his elfish grin, and I knew this was what he'd hoped I'd say. "It's the only way we'll know for sure," he confirmed. And then, a bit more ominously. "Some people choose to wait, but then there aren't many options if it spreads."

"I've decided," I repeated, and with that, he started an entirely different discussion. Once again, the picture was grim: Even if I did the second surgery, we weren't out of the woods.

The best case scenario was for the second surgery to be clear—no metastasis in my lymph nodes. This was a long shot and wasn't likely to would happen, but that's what we could hope for.

However, if the second surgery showed further metastasis in the lymph nodes—well, that situation wasn't good at all. That meant that cancer had spread to someplace place we couldn't find. Or I'd develop more melanomas in future, which was common.

We couldn't know any of this, until after the second surgery.

He spoke frankly and kindly, and suddenly my wall of reserve crumbled. Here was a man who dealt with death every single day. With his sparkling eyes and high vibration, I had the feeling he wouldn't judge me for my belief system, for the unique way I chose to look at the world.

Or, if he did … well, I could handle that, too.

And so, I told him.

I told him of the spiritual awakening that had brought about my psychic awakening years before. I told him of my work as a spiritual teacher and intuitive. I told him how I had worked with my mind and my body and my energy to move beyond fear and to live in high vibration, regardless of outcome. I told him I communicated with guides and angels, not just now and then, but regularly. I told him about the hemp oil.

Heck, I even told him about the carrots.

I told him about "only one," the message from my guides and I told him about my father's message of the "pearl of great price," and I told him I believe that the pearl was the micro-metastasis, and that it had already been removed.

I told him I also believed the price was my arm, and I was ready to do the second surgery, even though I didn't think it was necessary.

He listened, and he listened, and by the time I finished talking, the vibration in the room was so high, it felt more like a healing session than a medical meeting.

"Your story is fascinating," my oncologist said. "I haven't heard anything quite like this before." And then, as he turned to shake my hand, he smiled his bright, luminous smile and said the best words I could hope to hear:

"I don't expect to see you in this office again."

CHAPTER 28

Suffering

I WAS ONLY A WEEK POST OP and I hurt every day. I hurt so much I found it hard to do much of anything, except suffer. The top of my arm stung, the way skin stings if you pull it way, way too tight. My underarm was sliced open, and I had a drainage tube again; several feet of clear plastic tubing that emptied into a clear plastic suction bottle with a loop on top.

I couldn't take this drainage bottle off, even as it filled continuously with my own blood and fluid. One end of the tube went directly into my body, through a hole in my skin. In other words, I had to wear it 24/7.

I tried a variety of ways to attach this, but nothing worked well. In bed, I would roll on top of it. While resting, it bumped against my side, but no other bottle was available, and after a few days of having it bump around on my skin, I arranged to wear it on a ribbon around my neck.

Of course, the bottle didn't just hang there. It required maintenance: several times a day I was required to "strip" the long tube, squeezing all the blood and fluid away from the hole in my arm into the bottle.

Yuck.

Several times a day, I also needed to empty this bottle, and measure the amount of fluid in it. In this way, I could see if the drainage was slowing, or stopping.

I was not a happy person with this bottle of blood around my neck. In fact, of all indignities of surgery, this bothered me most.

It's not because I'm squeamish ... I'm not. I've been a mother to four kids for nearly 28 years. I have changed diapers, cleaned wounds, wiped up various bodily fluids for many others. But something about my own bodily fluids being stored outside my body disturbed me greatly.

It took all I had in me, not to pull the tubing out of my body.

In fact, it was so difficult to keep the tubing in, that I found myself beginning to cheat when I measured the amount of fluid collected in the bottle, jotting down slightly less than actually collected.

"It comes out when the drainage is under ten millimeters" my surgeon told me, and each day, I cheated just slightly on the actual number, trying to reach "ten" sooner. I knew this was detrimental to me.

And yet, I didn't stop myself.

Something about the tube meant I was still sick. I couldn't accept this thought; it didn't resonate with me.

Deep in the early days of my recovery, I understood I had a choice to be sick or I had a choice to be well. Everything in my intuitive self told me I was well— the first surgery had removed the micro-metastasis of cancer, and I was now cancer free. My pearl was gone.

But the price had to be paid. In seven days I would undergo a second surgery. I thought continually about the pearl and the price.

It was hard to face more pain.

Part Four

Surgery, Redux

CHAPTER 29

Surgery, Redux

I WAS SECOND IN THE LINEUP—the second operation my surgeon would perform that day.

We checked in at the main reception areas of the hospital this time, and that's when reality finally hit me: this was the big leagues. No simple day surgery this. Everything was bigger, newer, more organized. I had my own pre-op room, not a little curtained area. I had a nurse dedicated to only me, not shared by several other patients.

The seriousness of it all was unnerving, but by the time my nurse wrapped me in the standard cocoon of warm blankets, all my tears were gone and a certain calm had come over me.

Nothing beats having gone through the dress rehearsal to steady the nerves for the big event. This time, everything I noticed or experienced: the hospital bed, the monitors, the IV shunt, the way I'd have to drag along the IV stand if I wanted to use the bathroom ... all were familiar to me.

Plus, we were on some kind of fast track. No sooner had I climbed into my blankets then my anesthesiologist—a man this time—

breezed in, snapped open his file, and started through a lengthy list of questions.

"I had general anesthesia two weeks ago," I told him.

"Great!" he enthused, snapping my file shut. "We'll use what they used."

My surgeon flew in next, pumped up from the surgery he'd just finished. "I'm ready," I said, beating him to the punch.

This was like some hospital version of *Groundhog Day*, where everything happened the same, only slightly different.

Then the anesthesiologist started the drip and I packed away all my fears and put myself into an ecstatic state, calling in my guides and angels and my departed father and anyone else who wanted to help. My bed started to roll and I sailed down the hallway into another room, and this time I remember a mask being placed over my face, and the color blue, and light...

◆　◆　◆　◆

There would be no announcement at the end of this surgery. No "tissue clear" from my surgeon. This was a lymphadenectomy, a full removal of all the lymph nodes under my armpit.

We didn't know how many lymph nodes would be removed during this process; maybe six, maybe eleven maybe more. All of these would be meticulously checked and sampled at the micro level, in a pathology lab.

Either cancer would have metastasized to the nodes, which would be a disaster.

Or the tissue would be clear, which would be a miracle.

We wouldn't know the results for a few days.

CHAPTER 30

Dark Night

THE NIGHT I SPENT IN THE HOSPITAL still comes back to me in waves: an odd, dark, twisted dream where nothing makes sense.

I remember sending Steve home after realizing that the only place for him to sleep was an uncomfortable reclining chair. I remember my youngest daughter visiting me, brought in by her father for a quick hello.

I remember nurses, a parade of young women who stopped in to check my bandages, look at my monitors, and rearrange the various tubes and wires attached to all parts of my body, all the while asking me for psychic advice: this one was pregnant—would the baby be okay? That one just had twins—should she keep working? This one wanted to put her son in a better school—would that come to pass? That one needed to break up with her boyfriend—was he cheating on her?

I had to laugh. These nurses didn't know what I did for my work. Yet even in recovery, I was still an intuitive. I answered out of a haze of drugs, and I wasn't sure if I found it funny or sad to be doing psychic work from my hospital bed.

When we have found our true selves, we inhabit this self all the time. I found it interesting to learn this lesson right outside of surgery.

♦   ♦   ♦   ♦

In the early evening, a woman came in who was neither family member nor nurse. She had come from the church, the Catholic church, and said she'd come to pray with me. She pulled a tiny chest filled with the Host—holy communion—out of her purse.

I was confused. "I'm not a practicing Catholic," I said, thinking she'd gotten the wrong room.

"You're on the list," she said, peering at a sheet of paper. "You checked the box marked Catholic on your admission form."

I couldn't imagine this was so. I had been Catholic for many years, but I was no longer practicing.

"Okay…" I said. "It's just that … my beliefs have changed."

"Well, when was the last time you went to confession?" she asked. "Do you go to mass? What parish do you attend?"

No. No. None.

She wrinkled her nose.

And then, the definitive question: "Do you accept Jesus as your personal savior?"

I sighed. My mind was fuzzy, and I didn't think this would go well. "No. And yes. I love Jesus. Absolutely, completely." I stressed this, so she might understand. "But there is more. I love all the Divine beings, the holy ones, the ascended masters. The Universe is filled with this light."

She frowned.

"To me … the whole idea of God—well, it's way bigger than religion."

She was not happy with my answer. "Well, I can't give you communion if you're not a practicing Catholic," she snapped, and tucked the box with the Host back into her purse.

I suddenly felt very, very tired. I knew I couldn't explain to her what I felt, what I'd come to understand after all these mystic experiences and spiritual awakenings of the last few years, after all the messages I'd received, the people I'd worked with, and all the miracles I'd seen and would see.

"We could pray together," she finally offered uncertainly, "I guess that would be all right." And then to my great surprise, she got down on her knees on that cold, hard hospital floor, the surface likely swarming with all kinds of deadly germs, and she closed her eyes and pursed her lips together and started an Our Father, and I joined in.

When we were finished I crossed myself out of habit. I couldn't tell if this pleased her or not.

The rest of the night I had no further visitors. The pain seeped in and I buzzed the nurses for drugs. I remember watching what I think was *Lawrence Welk* on my room TV at 3:00 in the morning, but it might have been another show entirely.

I did not sleep that night. I lay in bed brimming with pain, flattened by drugs, with a mind that didn't work and an arm far more damaged than before.

In this manner, I waited for morning.

CHAPTER 31

Phone Call, Redux

MY SECOND SURGERY HAD BEEN ON a Friday. I came home from the hospital Saturday and spent the next few days in a drug-induced haze, my arm once again nested on a stack of pillows, a new suction bottle of blood and fluid hanging around my neck.

This time my bandages were much more elaborate. My arm hurt, but worse than that, it didn't feel right. The underside from elbow to armpit was totally numb—if I touched it, I couldn't feel a thing. The area from the armpit all the way down my side and into my breast felt swollen, puffy, and thick. Fluid had collected in all these areas, causing swelling throughout.

I felt as though my right arm was stuffed tight as a sausage with fluid, and if I hadn't checked its size several times a day, I would have believed my arm and side had swollen to be twice as big as my left.

When my cell phone rang Sunday morning, I didn't think too much about it. I get many phone calls, and usually let them go to voice mail. But something about this call seemed important. When I picked up, my surgeon was on the other end, and I felt my heart rise into my throat. This was either going to be very good or very bad news.

"I'm sorry to call you on the weekend," he said. "The lab results came back early."

I felt myself stop breathing.

"We took 13 lymph nodes," he said and his voice seemed to crack with some kind of strain. I didn't know what he was feeling, but suddenly something in his voice shifted and spiked.

"Thirteen lymph nodes, and all were clear." And then again: "All thirteen were clear!"

I almost fainted. Here I was in bed, the same place I'd been when I took the call telling me I had melanoma, but this time, I was hearing good news—miraculous news—that all was clear, the tissue was clear.

I felt astonished and grateful to realize everything my guides and my departed father had told me was true—there was "only one," a pearl of great price, the micro-metastasis that had been removed from my body in the first surgery.

I laughed, a little ruefully. Just as I'd thought, the second surgery hadn't been needed! And now my arm hurt like crazy, and would probably have problems forever.

And yet ... the tissue was clear.

I was cancer free.

This was the best-case scenario.

My surgeon, on the other end of the phone, was talking now, relaxed and happy. He was thrilled to have this result, to be part of this particular outcome. We laughed excitedly, and made plans for me to come in that week so he could check on the recovery.

Steve came into the room while I was still on the phone, and after I hung up he sat on the bed and held me. We laughed ... and we also cried.

Part Five

Integration

CHAPTER 32

Christmas

It's early in December, and we're putting up our tree.

What a year this has been—my mom almost dying, my daughter undergoing major scoliosis surgery, and now me, recovering from two cancer surgeries two weeks apart. Our Christmas tree marks the beginning of a return to normalcy, the first time we've been able to do something fun and ordinary in a long time.

We live in Oregon, in the literal heart of Christmas tree country. Thousands of fir trees surround us, not only growing wild on our property, but also planted in neat rows a few properties over. Most Christmases, the whole family piles into the car and we head to one of our neighbor's tree farms and spend an hour walking in the mud, and rain, trying to choose the perfect tree.

This year, none of us are up to it. I can barely use my arm, it's still swollen and numb and hurts day and night. I'm a wounded bird most days, not up for extra trips and outings. Instead, a friend who runs a nursery gives us this year's tree— already chopped and pruned and ready. The tree is perfect, even without the tradition, and Steve and my son tie it to the top of the car, while my daughter and I huddle together, two invalids still healing.

I'm excited to put up the tree and see all the old, familiar ornaments we've collected over the years. Some are unique—the "birds" Steve made for me the first Christmas we met, crafted from feathers and beach glass—beautiful, delicate fliers. The kids have their favorites, especially the ones they made when they were little made out of construction paper and glitter.

I open the box that contains the ornaments I especially love: a luminous golden angel, vintage and rare, and a golden eagle in remembrance of my father. I carefully hang those two ornaments upon the tree and then I realize, that's it. I can't do anything more this year.

I return to my pillow stack and sit on the sofa with my arm nested in the softness, watching Steve and my kids decorate the tree, and I call my oldest daughter on the phone, so she can join us.

As I'm watching, I notice a snowball ornament hung on the lower boughs—a perfectly round white ball—and I think to myself how much it resembles a pearl. A shiny pearl hanging on our tree, there to remind me of this Christmas, this year, and all we've been through and all we've learned.

The tree is fresh and fragrant, filling the entire house with light and warmth. I look at the people I love: Steve and my children, and I hold closely in my heart the others I love who are not here.

I'm so grateful to be alive. I'll take more Christmases, please, if I can get them. I lean back on the sofa, sink my swollen arm into the pillows, and enjoy what's now.

The snowball pearl bobs and sways on the lower branches as more ornaments are added. Today I am cancer free; considered cured by surgery. I do not know what the future will bring.

In truth, none of us do.

CHAPTER 33

Full Circle

I AM SWIMMING IN AN OUTDOOR POOL on the penthouse of a hotel in downtown Denver, while the sun hovers above—a bright white halo like a pearl in the sky. Beyond the tall glass windscreen that surrounds the pool, the reflective surfaces of multiple city high-rises wink back in the sun: they are modern in architecture, rising like great grey crystals: metallic, sturdy, new.

This afternoon dip in the pool is not for the faint of heart. The weather is cold in early February, and ice covers the tables and deck chairs poolside; ice lines the tiles that surround the pool; the cement is scattered with salt, and this also dazzles. In mid-winter, the pool water steams up from this icy expanse of cement like a misty, healing hot spring.

This is how I exist in Denver at this moment: with a great pearl of a winter's sun luminous overhead, ice on the ground, the pool steaming, and the water somehow so buoyant that I'm able to float with ease—I'm unsinkable in this warm, misting water.

I'm amazed by how I'm able to float in such stillness, without even my legs dragging to the bottom. Amazingly, my entire body remains afloat with no need to kick or struggle or even to flutter my hands. I am able to simply float here, no effort needed.

There is only being, experiencing, and allowing, here.

No effort required.

I float upon the water, an earth creature transformed somehow into an air creature, a sea creature—my eyes gazing into the blue sky, my body floating in the clear liquid. I am very much out of my element, here on the penthouse floor of a hotel in the middle of a modern cathedral city. And yet, I have never felt so relaxed.

I allow the stillness to support me, the water's gentle holding, and I realize my journey, such as it is, has come full circle.

◆　◆　◆　◆

Eight months earlier, when I first came to Denver, I didn't find myself floating in a pool with every cell of my body relaxed and easy. Back then, I was stressed and busy with my appearance at a promotional event—and it was back then, at a different hotel, wrapped in a fluffy white hotel towel, that I first noticed the mole on my shoulder—the tricky, brown black mole I knew was wrong from the moment I saw it.

Today I'm in the same city, but I'm in a different space altogether, here for the Denver Chant Fest, an event I'm attending for pure pleasure—no business involved. In an hour, I'll go to an ecstatic dance event, where I don't have to be a public figure in any way—I will go as myself only, my anonymous, private self, open to expand and enjoy whatever that experience brings. Later, I'll attend a kirtan, where I'll meditate and sing and be. My only purpose for this trip is to relax and enjoy.

As I look back at my life in these past eight months, I realize the truth of our lives: each life is a soul's journey taken in a human body. We're here to experience, we're here to learn, we're here to become closer to God and each other.

That's all.

I suspend my body once again in the deep buoyancy of the water, and I begin to meditate, still floating. I connect myself and my energy to the Universe, to the Divine/One/All, and scan my body carefully, to see if the cancer has come back, or if it is still there, and I listen to what my body has to tell me.

My body answers in chorus, each cell not like a flower, this time, but like an ocean of teeming plankton, an ocean of cells fully interconnected, connecting into the water, into the building, into the sky, into the earth, into the sky, beyond the atmosphere.

All is one.

I am at the heart of it, my whole body teeming with God.

There is no cancer today.

In this moment, I am healed.

I float in the comfort and the grace of this, and I understand that this feeling, this emotion, this sensation, this Divine infusion ... this is the place I can be at all times, whether or not I'm in a pool on the penthouse, or doing something else entirely.

I am always floating in the pool of the Universe, I am always floating in the water of the Divine.

There is nothing to do.

No effort is required.

All I need is to relax, enjoy, and surrender to this moment.

And after that ... surrender to the next.

♦   ♦   ♦   ♦

Cancer taught me great lessons—perhaps the most important soul lessons I will every learn:

- Cancer taught me to let go of fear—that fear and anxiety will never serve me.
- Cancer taught me to understand that mortality is reality, and the finite container of our lives gives them value and meaning.

- Cancer taught me to be in gratitude, for all the things and people I love.
- Cancer taught me that the Divine can heal anything in the body, in matter, in space—it's all possible, even if we don't understand how.

From cancer, I also learned that life is not meant to be rushed, pushed through, or gobbled up in order to get to the next piece faster. Life is to be savored. Every moment a miracle, the greatest blessing imaginable.

Every moment.

I still don't know if there's melanoma inside me that will spread, or if I will get melanoma again. Statistically, the chances are high, but I am not a statistic. I'm a living, breathing, Divine being in human form. It's my choice to connect with the Divine energy and to illuminate my own God self in every moment I remember to do so.

And when I forget, I may begin again, in this understanding.

You have this choice, also.

Regardless of whether you will be healed to live longer or whether you will transition from your journey because of cancer ... regardless of outcome, this moment is beautiful.

This moment.

Be in it, as fully as you are able. Nothing matters more than relaxing into what is—yourself as a Divine being in human body, floating in the reality of all.

Book Two

The Seven Meditations

HOW TO USE THE MEDITATIONS

THE EXPERIENCES I HAD DURING my journey with cancer—the visitations from spirit guides, the messages from my departed father, the Divine healing—are all easily available to you, if you choose to explore the path of spiritual intuition.

For this reason, I've created a series of seven simple meditations that will walk you through all the lessons I faced and the miracles I experienced, and allow you to experience these for yourself. The seven meditations are:

- Meditation One: Overcoming anxiety and fear
- Meditation Two: Tuning into the state of your body
- Meditation Three: Receiving healing from Divine guides and angels
- Meditation Four: Receiving support from departed loved ones
- Meditation Five: Healing your body at a cellular level
- Meditation Six: Shifting your vibration to gratitude and bliss
- Meditation Seven: Surrendering to the miracle of your Divine nature

You don't need special abilities to do these meditations and experience miracles in your life. In fact, I believe having cancer may actually expand your ability to connect deeply with the Divine in this way.

Please remember: your experience with these meditations will be different from anyone else's. What happens will depend on where you are in your cancer journey, and in your understanding of yourself as soul.

As I stated before, *these meditations are not meant to substitute for professional medical care;* as you can see from my own journey I relied heavily on traditional medicine to create my healing.

However, the meditations are amazing tools for creating spiritual and emotional healing, and for the possibility of creating healing miracles in your body.

Please also understand that, regardless of outcome, you have the ability to take charge of your emotional state, your attitude, and the way you understand the world as a conscious being. These meditations will help you achieve those things.

As a Divine being, as a soul, you have the ability to transcend your human life and live as you truly are—as a fully conscious presence, understanding the Universe in its most expanded and unlimited form. This is the gift of wisdom, available to anyone at any age, any stage of life—and it is yours simply for the asking.

♦ ♦ ♦ ♦

The meditations are easy to use. Simply read the information, hold it in your mind, then close your eyes, take a deep breath in through the nose and out through the mouth, and begin. If you prefer to use audio recordings for guided support, you'll find these at **www.sarawiseman.com**.

Here are a few answers to common questions:

Do the meditations have to be used in order?

No. There's no special order to them; you can use them in any sequence. Allow yourself to be drawn to what you need. For example, if you're struggling with fear, you'll want to use that meditation. If you long to connect with your guides and angels, use that meditation.

Do I need to do them in any time frame?

No. You can skip one, or repeat another as many times as you need. You can do one a day, or you can do one a week. Whatever works for you is right; and, whatever works for you during your illness is right. Trust yourself. Do what you can do, at the level you can do it.

Can the techniques here be used for diseases other than cancer?

Yes, absolutely. In fact, I encourage that. However, cancer has unique characteristics as opposed to other diseases. So, these practices and meditations have been created specifically with cancer in mind.

How were the meditations created?

I've been a teacher of spiritual intuition for many years now, and have worked with thousands of people using meditations like these. These are also the practices I used to create my own healing. I am happy to share them to you.

What if I do a meditation "wrong"?

You cannot do them wrong, in any way. That is not possible. Whatever you do will benefit you. Remember, the work of spiritual intuition has no hard and fast rules—we simply open to the presence that is One/All/God/Divine and are guided to do what we need to do. Simply open your heart and listen, and you will be informed.

Are these meditations from a certain religion?

No. These practices follow no creed or religion. The majority of my clients, when asked, say they believe in a higher power. Most were raised in traditional religions, but find these practices no longer are large enough to contain their understanding. A new way of thinking is coming into the world, based on the understanding of Oneness, and that reality is composed of many layers and levels we don't fully understand. In my own life I've had so much direct experience with angelic beings that I no longer react in disbelief when one arrives into my reality. Instead, I react in awe and gratitude.

Can I trust the information I receive in the meditations?

You may choose whether or not to believe in etheric entities and all the other holy beings that support us in all moments. At no time are these not with us. However, if you aren't used to sensing their presences, the experience can be unnerving.

When people say they don't believe in these beings, or they're not sure, I feel a sense of bemusement. Divine beings have been revered and recorded in our literature, music, and art for thousands of years, in all cultures, all traditions. These beings are not new to our planet, to our time, or to humanity. They have always been with us.

In any case, you'll need to discover your own beliefs for yourself, based on your experience with these practices. I know from my own experience how simple it is to move our consciousness into other realms and communicate with these beings—to go "beyond the veil" as some call it, or to "enter in" as I call it. I believe this is possible for all.

How were these meditations created?

My work in spiritual intuition began with a near death experience in 2000, during which for the first time I experienced a luminous presence I knew as God. I find it hard to explain this understanding; it was indescribably profound, and my life changed forever in those moments. Soon afterward, I experienced a spiritual and psychic awakening in which I began to understand life in a new way—my consciousness had begun to open. Cancer served as my second near death experience, and brought a continuation of the awakening that has now become my life's path.

How will the meditations help?

I invite you to experience the amazing peace and bliss that comes from communication with the Divine reality. Set aside your disbelief, or your feeling that this is not available to you, and allow these amazing beings to support you with their love and light. It is a comfort like no other, and when you allow yourself to bask frequently in this high vibration of the Divine, healing is possible and miracles become every day experiences.

Many of you reading this book will become cancer free; you will be cured by the sum of your efforts in traditional and holistic medicine, and intuitive healing. The opening of yourself to the Divine will benefit you for your entire life.

Others of you may not experience a cure, but that doesn't mean you will not experience miracles. When we're able to shift our minds from ordinary earth reality, into the Divine realm, we come to a different understanding of our lives, our purpose, and the soul lessons we're here to learn.

I invite you to set aside all reserve, fear, and uncertainty. Try the practices for yourself. The Divine is waiting for you. You have nothing to lose, and literally everything to gain.

Audio Support for the Meditations

Many people find it useful to use the audio version of these meditations as they "enter in." This can make the process easier, especially if you are new to meditation or spiritual intuition work. The audio version is available at **www.sarawiseman.com**

MEDITATION ONE

Overcoming anxiety and fear

...in which you relax the mind and its looping thoughts, replacing fear with peace.

CANCER ISN'T JUST A DISEASE OF THE BODY; it also affects the emotions. Even saying the word *cancer* brings us to a place of terror, resistance, and stress. When these feelings of low vibration take over, our the body loses its ability to hold immunity.

Thus, while the cancer cells are busy dividing and conquering, the mind begins to spin out into panic, right at the time when we most need to concentrate on holding a high vibrational state.

The first part of your healing begins when you stop existing in a fear state. This is not simple, but it is also not hard. The secret is to provide enough repetition so the brain's endless circling is interrupted when it goes into fear; we trick it into choosing another state.

You may find yourself doing this meditation more than any other meditation in this book. This one is perhaps the most important of the practices. You will be able to effectively raise your vibration out of the fear state, and then move into a place of peace and bliss, which is where healing happens.

Before you begin:

Contemplate these questions. You may answer them in journaling or in your mind. The answers may change as you move through your journey.

1. What do you most fear about cancer?
2. What else are you afraid of?
3. What do you need to be free of this fear? From other people? From yourself?

MEDITATION TO REPLACE FEAR WITH PEACE

Close your eyes, and take a deep breath in through the nose and out through the mouth. Take this deep breath again: in through the nose, and out through the mouth. Repeat this until you feel yourself relax into your body fully, so that you notice your chest beginning to expand, and your arms and legs feel heavy. As you transition into a state of relaxation, you may notice your body contracts, shudders, or adjusts for a moment or two as you release energy. And then, suddenly, you will notice a change: your body feels still, spacious, as if you're floating in water. You are so relaxed, it will be difficult to move.

You will notice you've relaxed in a way you do not normally experience. This state feels wonderful. In this state, you have no further need to pay attention to your breath; it takes care of itself. You have no need to pay attention to your body; it also takes care of itself.

♦ ♦ ♦ ♦

Now, keeping your eyes closed, I want you to scan your body, so you will notice where your body is holding fear. This may be where your cancer is located, or it may not. The fear may be centered in your head, throat, heart, or any other place on or in your body. The place your body is holding fear may be different every time you do this meditation.

Simply notice where the fear is located; if it's in your torso, or your back, or your skin, or wherever you find it. Simply notice it. The fear may even be outside your body at this time. Simply notice it, and you will begin to see how the fear presents as a filmy, grayish black, muddy brown, dark green, or yellow color. Fear may appear as a hazy shadow. This may also be different each time you do the meditation. Simply notice the color and texture of your fear, today. Try to describe this to yourself in your mind, such as: my fear today is black and gritty. Or, my fear today is yellowish and smoky.

Now, you'll begin to ask this fear, this clustering of energy you have noticed, to coalesce or come together, so it begins to pull away from your body and form itself into a separate shape, such as a grey ball or cloud, away and apart from your body. Ask the fear to do this. If it does not do this at first, ask your angels and Divine guides to assist you in this task, and it will be done before you finish asking. Trust this. You are never alone in this process.

As this dark ball or cloud separates from your body and begins to float or hover in front of you, allow yourself to recognize it as your fear. You may say in your mind: this is my fear, separate from myself.

Now, ask your fear, what is would like you to know today. You may find a memory floats into your mind, or you may think of a person, or you may have a thought or a vision. This information will arrive instantaneously to you; you do not have to "work" or "try" to get it. It will just show up. When this information comes into your mind, don't push it away. Invite it to continue. Treat it like a thread or path you follow. Ask it to "tell you more," or "show you more."

For example, if a memory comes into your mind, go back into that memory and linger there a bit. Ask to recall it more clearly and to be shown what this memory is trying to tell you. Often, our fears are built upon old memories from our lives; your current fear may be related to something that happened long ago.

Also, listen to any phrases or words that come to you. Look for any images that suddenly pop into your head. Simply ask the fear to show you more, tell you more, until you understand what this message is.

Once you have some idea of what your fear is, allow it to be replaced by higher vibration energy.

To do this, imagine a golden ball of luminous light is gently floating toward you. The light may arrive from the right, the left, above, or below. You will suddenly begin to notice it in your mind. As it floats toward you, the light will begin engulfing the energy that is your fear. Soon, all that is floating toward you has turned to a golden, luminous glowing ball or cloud. The light will absorb or replace the fear energy.

Understand, this is Divine energy. Fear cannot exist in this state of high vibration.

Allow this Divine energy to tell you what you need to know right now, about staying out of fear. You may hear a phrase, a word, or have a sudden understanding. You may feel the presence of peace. You may receive a vision in your mind, or a deep knowing. Allow all these feelings to flow within you.

Bring this golden radiance toward you; it will come easily. Allow this golden energy to fill your body completely, not just in the place where the fear was, but throughout your body. Center this energy over your heart and allow it to permeate your heart.

Rest in this magnificence and peace, for as long as you like.

When you are ready, return to earth reality by slowly counting backwards from ten, nine, eight, seven, six, five, four, three, two, one. The peaceful feeling will stay with you. You will be back in the room, fully present.

♦　♦　♦　♦

Repeat this meditation as often as you need, especially when you're beginning to learn how to release your fear. In time, you will become so adept at this meditation, you will be able to do it anywhere: while resting, at a doctor's office, or during a treatment— any time you need help.

MEDITATION TWO

Tuning into the state of your body

...in which you check in with your body on an energetic level to see what healing is in progress.

WHEN YOU'RE HEALING FROM CANCER, it's useful to be able to take a look at what's going on in your body. With this meditation, we aren't trying to change anything; we're simply looking at what's happening—at what our bodies want us to know.

As you check in with your body using intuition, you will begin to notice what may be different from the last time you checked, what is healed, what is healing, and what still needs to be healed. These are useful things to know when you're facilitating healing.

Before you begin:

Contemplate the following questions. You may answer them in journaling or in your mind. The answers may change as you move through your journey.

1. What is the most recent information from your physician about what's happening in your body?

2. Does this seem correct to you intuitively? If not, what seems incorrect or different?

3. How do you feel today, in general? How do you feel overall, on a scale of one to ten, with ten being perfect health?

4. What parts of your body don't feel good? What parts of your body feel neutral? What parts feel good?

MEDITATION ON THE STATE OF YOUR BODY

Close your eyes and take a deep breath in through the nose and out through the mouth. Take this deep breath again: in through the nose, and out through the mouth. Repeat this until you feel yourself relax into your body fully, so you notice your chest begins to expand and your arms and legs feel heavy. As you transition into a state of relaxation, you may notice your body contracts, shudders, or adjusts for a moment or two as you release energy, and then suddenly you will notice a change: your body will feel still, spacious, as if you are floating in water. You will feel so relaxed, it will be difficult to move.

You will notice you've relaxed in a way that you do not normally experience. It feels wonderful. In this state, you have no further need to pay attention to your breath; it takes care of itself. You have no need to pay attention to your body; it also takes care of itself.

♦ ♦ ♦ ♦

Now I want you to notice something wonderful hovering near your body; it has the appearance of a gentle, luminous wand of light. You may notice an angel or Divine being is holding this wand, or it may be floating in the air. Either way is fine.

As you relax, this gentle, comforting, and luminous wand light will begin scanning your body—it will hover over you, stopping at any part of your body that needs to be examined more fully.

This wand may stop or hover at any place on your body—not necessarily where your cancer is located. Every time this wand stops over an area you will feel a sense of questioning, or considering. All you need to do is allow your attention to focus on this part of your body for a moment, letting information to come into your mind. This may be an image, a vision, an idea, a thought, a memory, or a feeling. For example, if you see images of a water pitcher, waterfall, or water, you may understand your body is asking for more hydration. If you see pictures or get the idea of cakes, cookies, and sweets and you have the idea of your blood, you be receiving information about your sugar levels, or even diabetes.

At other times, the wand will hover over areas where there is an emotional issue rather than a physical problem. For example, if the wand stops at your heart and you're suddenly reminded of your daughter who just left home for college, this may help you to recognize the feeling of sorrow, loss, or grieving you hold in your heart.

Allow yourself to be present to emotional aspects, as well as the physical. They are all related. Our body is merely a container of energy, and emotional responses affect this energy.

If you don't know what the wand of light wants you to examine, simply ask it to clarify. You don't need medical knowledge to become clear on what the wand is saying. Simply ask it. Notice what thoughts come into your mind and trust that you will understand.

Now, ask your body these questions:

Where does my body need help?

What help is needed?

What else do I need to know?

Allow yourself to notice what comes into your mind, and then proceed to the end of each thought thread, however it arrives: as words, message, idea, vision, emotion. All methods are useful.

When you feel this meditation is complete and you've gathered all the intuitive information available for today, simply bring yourself back to earth reality by slowly counting back from ten, nine, eight, seven, six, five, four, three, two, one. You will be back in the room and your earth reality, fully present.

♦ ♦ ♦ ♦

You can do this meditation daily, or you can do it now and then, such as before or after a doctor's appointment. Once you begin to become familiar with the state of your body, it will be easy to notice changes.

If you are given information during your meditation, such as "stop eating sweets" or "release your grief," please pay attention. Spiritual intuition provides information beyond our rational understanding, and what you receive in these meditations may be critical information for you.

MEDITATION THREE

Receive healing from Divine guides and angels

...in which you communicate with angels, guides, ascended masters, saints, holy ones and other etheric beings.

ONCE YOU UNDERSTAND HOW TO communicate with the etheric beings that continually surround and support us, you will never feel the same again. However, there's no point proceeding with this meditation until you're willing to accept the possibility that Divine beings exist, and that the layers and levels of the universe are in fact filled with entities of all kinds.

In recent years, many experts and highly educated people have been racing to write books about their experiences, including surgeons and physicians who in the past would have contested the existence of "heaven," "angels" and other entities. This is not new information—just new to our time and culture. The similarities in these expert tales match the stories written centuries ago by mystics, yogis, saints, spiritual teachers, and ordinary people who had miraculous experiences. Angels are indeed among us.

♦　♦　♦　♦

The entities you meet in this mediation will be especially concerned with helping you heal from cancer. They may give you information about test results or treatments. They may perform an energetic healing for you. They may have other information for you.

Feel free to ask them questions; bring all your concerns to them, for they are Divine and support you in every way.

Your angels and guides may feel familiar to you. This is because many of them have been with you since before you were born, for many lifetimes. In Christian terms, you might know these entities as "guardian angels," in another language, as "guides." The names are not important. All manner of Divine beings may be available to you—angels, guides, saints, holy ones, and ascended masters. Be open to this possibility. Entities may also appear as animals, such as shamanic totems, or even as living beings, such as tree spirits, and so on.

Before you begin:

Contemplate these questions. You may answer them in journaling, or in your mind. The answers may change as you move through your journey.

1. Do you remember having contact with angelic beings or other Divine entities as a child?
2. Have you had a near death experience or other trauma or miracle in which your spiritual self was opened and you experienced the Divine?
3. Do your spiritual beliefs allow you to communicate with Divine beings?
4. Are you willing to explore the possibility that Divine beings exist, and that it is easy to reach them for help in your cancer journey? If you answer yes, please continue with the meditation. If you answer no or you aren't sure, please postpone this mediation until you are certain.

MEDITATION TO REACH DIVINE BEINGS

Close your eyes and take a deep breath in through the nose and out through the mouth. Take this deep breath again: in through the nose, and out through the mouth. Repeat this until you feel yourself relax into your body fully, so you notice your chest begins to expand and your arms and legs feel heavy. As you transition into state of relaxation, you may notice your body contracts, shudders or adjusts for a moment or two as you release energy. Suddenly you will notice a change: your body will feel still, spacious, as if you are floating in water. You will be so relaxed, it will be difficult to move.

You will notice you have relaxed in a way you do not normally experience. It feels wonderful. In this state you have no further need to pay attention to your breath; it takes care of itself. You have no need to pay attention to your body; it also takes care of itself.

◆ ◆ ◆ ◆

Now, imagine you see a doorway in your mind's eye, and as you view this doorway further, you recognize it's an elevator door. You notice a glowing button to your right. Push this button now.

The doors will gently slide open and you will enter this elevator, which is actually an energetic portal to the place where it is easiest for you to reach your Divine guides and angels. There are other ways to reach this place of higher vibration; this is just one of them. We are using an elevator, because it is easy for you to imagine.

Check to see if any entities are already waiting inside the elevator with you; this is effortless, you will just "know" they are with you, or that you're by yourself. Either way is fine. The elevator is clean and bright. You feel relaxed there.

There are three buttons on the wall: 1, 2 and 3. You rise through the floors, passing level two, happy to be going to a new destination, a new layer or level of the Universe. As you arrive at level three, you find yourself relaxing even more, yet at the same time you also feel a sense of transition, as if you are entering a higher elevation or altitude. This is how you feel when your vibration shifts to a higher level. You may feel your chest expand, your body contract. This is fine. There are no worries as you do this. All is well.

As you notice the elevator rising to level three, you begin to feel saturated with Divine energy. As the elevator doors open you realize you have reached your destination: the layer or level where it is easiest for Divine beings to communicate with you.

You step outside the elevator into a new reality. For some of you, this may be a beautiful natural setting. For others, a bright, light space. You may have a different experience each time you do this meditation, and each time you will find yourself exactly where you need to be.

As you step outside the elevator, the beings will step with your, or you will notice beings coming toward you. You will sense their presence in your mind's eye; they may appear to be glowing with light, or luminous. You begin to identify simple characteristics about them, such as: short or tall, male or female, what they might be wearing, or carrying. These will be angelic beings, spirit guides, saints, or ascended masters. It is common to see Jesus, Mother Mary, and other holy ones. You will easily understand who they are.

This being or beings will have a message for you, or an answer to a question that has been in your mind or in your heart. Allow yourself to receive this message now. It may arrive as word, thought, telepathy, a voice in your head that is not yours, or a deep knowing. Sometimes the being may present you with an object; this may be symbolic. Sometimes the message is simple, such as "trust" or "all is well." Sometimes it is specific, such as information about your cancer or treatments. You may safely reveal everything to these beings of Divine love, for they already know what is in your heart.

When you feel this meditation is complete and you have gathered all the intuitive information available for today, bring yourself back to earth reality, by slowly counting back from ten, nine, eight, seven, six, five, four, three, two, one. You will be back in the room, in your earth reality, fully present.

♦   ♦   ♦   ♦

You can do this meditation daily, or do whenever you desire the clarity, comfort, and peace these beings provide. If you are given information during your meditation, please take note and allow yourself to trust it.

MEDITATION FOUR

Receiving support from departed loved ones

…in which you are supported by those who have loved you dearly, and who continue to love you.

OUR ANCESTORS CONTINUALLY SUPPORT us beyond the veil after they have departed this particular life. I was fortunate enough to know my father during this lifetime, and he supported me when we were living. He also supported me after he passed.

This is also true of your ancestors, whether or not you had the opportunity to know them in person. In fact, it is also true of your ancestors, whether you liked them or not!

I have found in my intuitive work with clients that even parents, siblings, grandparents, and other family members support us in this lifetime, even if we did *not* have wonderful relationships when they were alive. This is because moving beyond the veil, or into the next lifetime, brings about a shift in consciousness from petty concerns into love and a greater understanding of the universe and all its light.

In almost every case where I've worked with the departed for clients, they are loving and supportive. If there were problems in the relationship, the departed usually show up with contrition to say, "I'm sorry," and, "I love you."

Sometimes, if the death happened under extraordinary circumstances—such as suicide or a sudden accident, the soul will be conflicted or tormented. But in most cases, the departed will be quite different than when they were living: more loving and open, with a much higher level of consciousness.

Thus, you can call upon ancestors and family members who have passed in order to receive messages from them. Even if you aren't sure how to contact them, or aren't certain you want to reach them, they may be actively trying to contact you. This may take the form of dreams, visions, scents, sensations, and more concrete physical signs such as meaningful objects being moved or placed into spots where you might notice them.

How the contact comes isn't important—whether it's something you are actively seeking, or something that arrives on its own. For example, often the departed arrive to us in vivid dreams with such clear messaging that you remember them all day. The message of the dream is often crystal clear—you understand immediately what the departed is trying to tell you. Other times, the dream brings with it the emotion of extreme comfort, care, safety, or support.

Sometimes, the departed will be able to work with our reality to the extent of setting up a synchronistic event or happening. For example, you may be thinking about your departed grandmother, and then the next day you find the ring that she gave you somehow moved from your jewelry box into a drawer. When you open the drawer, you immediately see the ring. You feel a strong sense that your grandmother is with you, and all is well.

My father came to me frequently during my cancer journey; your departed loved ones are also there to support you. Do the meditation and be aware that this miracle can happened for you.

Before you begin:

Contemplate these questions. You may answer them in journaling, or in your mind. The answers may change as you move through your journey.

1. Who are the departed people in your life that you would most like to contact. Name them now.
2. Have you had the experience of seeing ghosts, spirits or being in contact in any way with the departed? Write about it or recall it now.
3. Do your spiritual beliefs allow you to communicate with departed loved ones?
4. Are you willing to explore the possibility that you can contact departed loved ones for help in your cancer journey? If you answer yes, please continue with the meditation. If you answer no or you aren't sure, please postpone this mediation until you are certain.

MEDITATION TO REACH DEPARTED LOVED ONES

Close your eyes, and take a deep breath in through the nose and out through the mouth. Take this deep breath again: in through the nose, and out through the mouth. Repeat this until you feel yourself relax into your body fully, so notice that your chest begins to expand and your arms and legs feel heavy. As you transition into state of relaxation, you may notice your body contracts, shudders or adjusts for a moment or two as you release energy, and then suddenly you will notice a change: your body will feel still, spacious, as if you're floating in water. You will be so relaxed, it will be difficult to move.

You will notice you have relaxed in a way you do not normally experience. It feels wonderful. In this state, you have no further need to pay attention to your breath; it takes care of itself. You have no need to pay attention to your body; it also takes care of itself.

♦   ♦   ♦   ♦

We will use the elevator again; this is an easy way for you to enter into the layer, or level, of guides, angels, and the departed.

Notice yourself now in front of the elevator door. the doors gently slide open and you enter this elevator. Check to see if any entities are already waiting inside with you; this is effortless, you will just "know" they are with you, or that you're by yourself. Either way is fine.

There are three buttons on the wall: 1, 2 and 3. You rise through the floors, passing level two, happy to be going to a new destination, a new layer or level of the Universe. As you arrive at level three, you find yourself relaxing even more, yet at the same time you also feel a sense of transition, as if you're entering a higher elevation or altitude. This is how you feel when you vibration shifts to a higher level. You may feel your chest expand, your body contract. This is fine. There are no worries as you do this. All is well.

As you notice the elevator rising to level three, you begin to feel saturated with Divine energy. As the elevator doors open you realize you have reached your destination: the layer or level where it is easiest for Divine beings to communicate with you.

You step outside the elevator door into a new reality. As you step outside the elevator, you will notice a spirit guide, angel, or other Divine entity coming toward you. You may recognize this entity from your last meditation, or this entity may be familiar to you. You will notice this Diving being has no message for you this time; they are there to hold space, and to hold vibration.

Every time you enter into this layer or level of the Universe, you will remember that a Divine being must accompany you, in order to hold the vibration required to enter this realm.

Now, you will notice other beings to the sides of your awareness: these are the departed. You may have a sense of a small gathering, or people trying to reach you. Some you may recognize, others may just appear as beings.

One being will come out from the crowd and move in front of you. This will likely be the departed loved one you would most like to contact, or another departed who can speak for this person. Take notice of who this is, and also notice how easy it is for you to recognize them. Notice the clothing they wear, and the age at which they appear.

This departed being will have a message for you—it may not arrive as easily as it did with the guides or angels; it may seem more like a pantomime, an action to show you something, a symbolic object,symbolic, or something else. You may receive the message from the departed in your mind, as words or a knowing.

Simply converse in a normal fashion and allow yourself to receive information, support, and love. Stay in this connection for as long as you like. It is normal to feel emotional, to cry, to be affected and touched by this meeting. You will also feel great relief to know the departed are not gone from our lives forever, but are eternally available to us at all times.

When this departed loved one seems to be finished, notice if one more being who would like to converse with you. Allow this communication as well. At all times, your guide or angel will be with you, holding space and holding the highest vibration for this encounter.

If for some reason no departed being appears, ask your guide for assistance. If at any time you feel uncomfortable or unsure, ask your guide for help.

When you feel this meditation is complete and you have gathered all the intuitive information available for today, bring yourself back to earth reality by slowly counting back from ten, nine, eight, seven, six, five, four, three, two, one. You will be back in the room, in your earth reality, fully present.

♦ ♦ ♦ ♦

You can do this meditation from time to time, or whenever you desire the clarity, comfort, and peace being with a departed loved one provides. If you receive information during your meditation, please take note and allow yourself to trust it.

MEDITATION FIVE

Healing your body at a cellular level

…in which you connect to your body at cellular level and request Divine healing.

You ARE NOT SEPARATE FROM your body. As a Divine being, you and your cells are one and the same. It is entirely possible to connect deeply with your body at a cellular level and use Divine energy to create change, healing, and miracles in your body. When we work in the highest vibration with the Divine, anything is possible.

This meditation shows you how to make the connection.

Before you begin:

Contemplate these questions. You may answer them in journaling, or in your mind. The answers may change as you move through your journey.

1. Do you believe you can create energy healing at the cellular level?

2. Are you ready to shift the energy in your body at a cellular level, right now?

3.   Do you believe energy healing is a reality?

4.   Do you believe miracles exist?

If you answer yes to these questions, please continue with the meditation. If you answer no, please postpone this meditation until a later time, when you are ready.

MEDITATION FOR ASKING YOUR CELLS TO HEAL

Close your eyes and take a deep breath, in through the nose and out through the mouth. Take this deep breath again: in through the nose, and out through the mouth. Repeat this until you feel yourself relax into your body fully, so that notice that your chest begins to expand, and your arms and legs feel heavy. As you transition into state of relaxation, you may notice that your body contracts, shudders or adjusts for a moment or two as you release energy, and then suddenly you will notice a change: your body will feel still, spacious, as if you are floating in water. You will feel so relaxed, it will be difficult to move.

You will notice you've relaxed in a way you don't normally experience. This relaxation feels wonderful. In this state you have no further need to pay attention to your breath; it takes care of itself. You have no need to monitor your body; it also takes care of itself.

♦   ♦   ♦   ♦

Now, begin to pay attention to your body. You may use the wand of energy or light as you did in the earlier meditation, or you may tune into what your body would like you to know, by scanning all parts of your body and noticing areas of difference.

In your mind's eye, scan your body slowly from head to neck, chest to belly. Move from torso to arms, hands, legs, feet. Move from front to back. Notice all the parts of your body, and see if any areas call for your attention.

Your attention may be called to areas where you have cancer, or are healing from cancer, or your attention may be called to different areas. Look at the different areas first. Simply notice the spots that call for your attention. Notice if this is a part of the body, or a body system. Ask this part of your body what it would like you to know.

You may experience memories, thoughts, or ideas; you may see visions or receive other information at this time, just as you did in the previous meditation.

Focus on all the parts of your body you are noticing, and allow the information to come to you as it will, until this feels complete.

Now, turn your attention to parts of your body where cancer is currently residing. Do not worry about communicating or talking to the cancer cells in your body. Instead, concentrate on the cells you notice that are involved with the cancer.

Do not worry if you cannot identify these cells. This is not important. Instead, simply ask these cells to show you, via memory, image, vision, symbolism or "movie in your head" how they are doing. These cells are part of your body; they are completely and utterly you. You have the ability to talk or communicate with these cells, because they are also you.

Talk to them now.

Ask them to show you how they are doing.

Ask what support they need.

Ask them to show you in a vision, metaphor, symbol, story, memory, movie ... however the cells will find it easiest for you to understand. Allow this information to arrive to you now.

Now, ask your cells how they are doing in keeping the cancer in a certain place, i.e. not spreading. Ask them how they are doing in eliminating the cancer.

Again, ask your cells, or whatever image that symbolizes your cells, to tell you.

For example, in my case, I received the image first of my cells as flowers, and then of my cells as samurais fighting in a battle. You may receive an image of your cells that is similar, or very different. The image will be appropriate to your situation and your healing.

Now, ask your cells to place all their effort toward healing, and ask them to show you in advance how this will look and feel. As you watch and notice what happens, understand your cells are showing you a future possibility of healing.

See this image, feel it, and know it.

Tell your cells this is the outcome or result you would like.

Ask them to create this for you.

Notice your cells' response. Is there is anything you need to do, or shift, or change in your life, for your cells to do this for you? Are they working toward this already? Is it unclear what is happening? Allow yourself to fully receive this information.

Now, some of you will also notice that Divine beings are beginning to show up in your meditation. Some of you may notices angels and guides or other entities who are capable of healing. The departed may show up, but they are not capable of creating healing for you; only higher level entities can do this work.

Some of you may notice what you may recognize as Divine "medical teams," or groups of entities who appear ready to work on, or in, your body. Allow this healing if you like. It is common to feel the guides working on you with light, energy, tools, or light objects you don't recognize, and to feel some shifting or response in the areas they are working on.

For example, you may have the idea they are removing something unneeded, or doing a "psychic surgery" in which they rearrange or reattach or correct something. This sounds odd, but when you're in the experience of meditation, it's common to feel and notice these things happening on a Divine or energetic level.

Sometimes your guides will focus light or Divine energy in the areas that need healing. Or, you may have your own experience. Having an emotional reaction is normal when the guides are doing this type of intensive energy healing. Allow your emotions to express as sound, convulsions, shakes or shuddering, crying, and so forth—whatever you need to do, or whatever your body does on its own.

When the healing is complete, you will feel different. Check in with your cells at this time, to see if they would like to tell you or show you something new. In many cases, the energy of your body will feel completely different to you after this kind of Divine healing.

When you feel this meditation is complete and you have gathered all the intuitive information available for today, bring yourself back to earth reality, by slowly counting back from ten, nine, eight, seven, six, five, four, three, two, one. You will be back in the room, in your earth reality, fully present.

♦　♦　♦　♦

You can do this meditation daily, if you like, or less frequently if you find the experience too intense. Also, when you begin to heal, you will notice you sense or see immediate changes whenever you enter in to talk with your cells—you will have the feeling of "my cancer is gone," or "my cancer is receding." Trust this; trust what your body tells you. If your cells aren't providing you with this information yet, continue to go in and communicate with your cells, asking them, "tell me more," or "show me more."

MEDITATION SIX

Shifting your vibration to gratitude and bliss

...in which you acknowledge your life as a miracle.

WHEN WE ARE ABLE TO LOOK AT our lives as finite containers, we realize that our experiences are inexpressively amazing. Existing as Divine beings in human bodies, living the years of our lifespan, having relationships with others, and the understanding we gain: each of these is a miracle.

In this meditation, we call your attention once again to the miracle that is your life on earth.

Before you begin:
Contemplate these questions. You may answer them in journaling or in your mind. The answers may change as you move through your journey.

1. What are the soul lessons you believe you have already learned in your lifetime?
2. What are the soul lessons you are currently working on?

3. What has your cancer experience taught you so far?
4. What lessons do you need help in learning?

MEDITATION ON YOUR LIFE AS A MIRACLE

Close your eyes, and take a deep breath in through the nose and out through the mouth. Take this deep breath again: in through the nose, and out through the mouth. Repeat this until you feel yourself relax into your body fully, so you notice your chest begins to expand and your arms and legs feel heavy. As you transition into state of relaxation, you may notice your body contracts, shudders or adjusts for a moment or two as you release energy, and then suddenly you will note a change: your body will feel still, spacious, as if you are floating in water. You will feel so relaxed, it is difficult to move.

You will notice you've relaxed in a way you don't normally experience. It feels wonderful. In this state you have no further need to pay attention to your breath; it takes care of itself. You have no need to pay attention to your body; it also takes care of itself.

♦ ♦ ♦ ♦

Now, begin to remember your life. Start at the beginning, from the moment you were born. You may think you don't have the ability to remember this, but when you're in a state of deep relaxation, as you are now, memories will arrive that you recognize as yours. Begin moving forward in your life, as if you are seeing a movie of your life in fast forward.

Some of the experiences in your life were not positive; however, as you review them now you'll notice the memories you receive have a different feeling, as if you're watching yourself from a soul perspective, not just from the perspective of yourself as a human. You will notice that when you look at your life from a soul perspective, things seem different.

Some of the experiences in your life may be extraordinary, astonishing, awe producing, and inspiring. You may remember love, beauty, peace, happiness, and bliss at a new level as you move through your life memories in this way. In each instance of such shocking gratitude, awe and bliss, you may find yourself having an emotional response as you experience the memory. Allow this, fully. It is normal to cry, shudder, rock, exclaim, or experience bliss as you journey in this way.

Move through your lifetime: infancy, toddler stage, childhood, teenage years, young adult, adulthood, and so forth. If you wish, you may also choose to see memories of what is to come: you are able now to see the future in your mind. Ask your mind to show you this, and experience this fully.

You will notice it is easy to move back and forth in your timeline of memories if the Divine would like you to look at something more deeply, or understand it more fully. Do this now, as many times as you wish, as you begin to see, remember, and understand the miracle of your life.

When you feel this meditation is complete and you have gathered all the intuitive information available for today, bring yourself back to earth reality, by slowly counting back from ten, nine, eight, seven, six, five, four, three, two, one. You will be back in the room, in your earth reality, fully present.

◆ ◆ ◆ ◆

You can do this meditation from time to time, when you require clarity or require a spiritual view of your life's meaning. If you are given information during your meditation, please take note and allow yourself to trust it.

MEDITATION SEVEN

Surrendering to the miracle of your Divine nature

...in which you discover your true essence as Divine, and your true state as peace.

THE PURPOSE OF LIFE IS SOUL GROWTH. Once we understand ourselves as Divine beings, as souls, and grasp the eternity of our souls' existence, we are able to understand the meaning of our lifetime on earth in a new way.

For most people this is not an understanding that comes quickly or easily. But when it does arrive to you, you will feel a sense of completion and peace. All suddenly becomes clear, and you no longer have worry or concern for what the next year, month, day, or even minute will bring. All of it is Divine.

At this level of consciousness you understand on the soul level that all is well, all is always perfect, through Divine grace and love.

This level of consciousness arrives to many folks who are journeying through cancer. Illness is often a great opener into awakening.

♦   ♦   ♦   ♦

Before you begin:
Answer the following questions, in journaling or in your mind.

1. If it was your Divine path to die from cancer, could you accept this? There is no right answer. Just simply notice what your answer is today.

2. Do you feel you have accomplished what you wanted in your life? The things you needed to do?

3. Is there anything further you need to complete or heal before you die? There is no right answer. Simply notice what your answer is today.

4. Do you believe all is well, regardless of what happens to you? Again, there is no right answer. Simply notice your response.

MEDITATION ON YOUR TRUE ESSENCE

Close your eyes and take a deep breath, in through the nose and out through the mouth. Take this deep breath again: in through the nose, and out through the mouth. Repeat this until you feel yourself relax into your body fully, so you feel your chest begin to expand, and your arms and legs feel heavy. As you transition into a state of relaxation, you may notice your body contracts, shudders, or adjusts for a moment or two as you release energy, and then suddenly you will note a change: your body will feel still, spacious, as if you are floating in water. You are so relaxed, it will be difficult to move.

You will notice you've relaxed in a way that you do not normally experience. It feels wonderful. In this state, you have no further need to pay attention to your breath; it takes care of itself. You have no need to pay attention to your body; it also takes care of itself.

♦ ♦ ♦ ♦

Now, ask to see yourself as a soul. You may notice this begin to happen in different ways, but one way many people see the soul is a flame of light; an infinite energy presence.

Recognize yourself as this flame of light, and allow yourself to receive the information you are already familiar with at this level: that your soul would like your human aspect to understand. This is information you already know. Remember, you are a Divine being—a soul—in human body. This information is entirely familiar to you; recognizing what you know is a matter of shifting your perspective from human, to Divine. Do this now.

Recognize yourself as this infinite flame of light; you are a piece of God/One/All that is not just a part, but a whole Universe.

You do not just have God/One/All within you; you are That.

Your soul is not just a piece of God/One/All; it is all That.

This is the true nature of your soul, and all souls.

Recognize this now. Hold this idea of God/One/All as not separate, not distinct, but as you—eternal soul of light and love.

Understand that as soul, your true essence, nothing can harm or hurt you; all is well, perfect, and Divine in all moments, in this existence and all others. This is the true nature of your being.

Some of you may find this understanding new. Allow yourself to consider it as possibility, and notice what happens when you allow this. If you have accepted this understanding already, simply stay in this consciousness and notice what happens as you experience it further.

Allow yourself to stay in this state, in this understanding, for as long as you desire.

When you feel this meditation is complete, bring yourself back to earth reality, by slowly counting back from ten, nine, eight, seven, six, five, four, three, two, one. You will be back in the room, in your earth reality, fully present.

♦ ♦ ♦ ♦

You can do this meditation whenever you need the comfort and peace of remembering your true reality. If you are given information or experience a shift in consciousness or understanding during your meditation, please take note and allow yourself to trust it.

ABOUT THE AUTHOR

In 2000, Sara Wiseman had a near death experience that created a spiritual and psychic opening—and change her life forever. Since that time, she has written numerous books on spiritual intuition, Divine healing, and has taught thousands of students how to create a direct connection to Divine/One/All. In 2012, Sara was diagnosed with melanoma; this experience led to the furthering of her awakening and expansion of her writing and teaching on spiritual intuition, energy healing and miracles.

Sara hosts the popular *Ask Sara* and *Sanctuary* radio shows and blog, is a top contributor to *DailyOM*, and has released four healing CDs with her band Martyrs of Sound. She works privately and in groups with clients worldwide.

For more information and to contact her, please visit

www.sarawiseman.com

Audio Support

For this book, Sara Wiseman has created the *Intuition, Cancer & Miracles* companion audio book, a series of seven guided meditations accompanied by healing music from her award-winning band Martyrs of Sound.

This audio course can make it easier for you to follow along with the meditations. To order, visit her website below.

Sara Wiseman also offers a variety of audio courses to complement her teachings and books, as well as free podcasts from her popular radio shows *Ask Sara* and *Sanctuary*.

For complete information, visit **www.sarawiseman.com**

BOOKS BY THE AUTHOR

Living a Life of Gratitude
Your Journey to Grace, Joy, and Healing

When you walk through life with gratitude, simply appreciating everything—every single thing—you reconnect with what's truly important in life. The awe and wonder of life is now ever present.

Through 88 illuminating short stories, *Living a Life of Gratitude* will help you slow down, look around, and see your life for what it is. From our first breaths to our last, Sara Wiseman explores the landmarks of human experience: that we are able to be children and have children, that we can learn and love! Even if we have little, we have so much. Read this book, and revel in the beauty of the world.

978-0-738737-53-9, 384 pp., 5 x 7 $16.99

The Four Passages of the Heart

Moving from Pain into Love

What if spiritual awakening rested within your own heart? What if you could heal past wounds and create a life of joy, simply via heart's opening? In this transformational book, Sara Wiseman busts the myth that change work is slow and the path to happiness is difficult. In reality, spiritual awakening is part of who we are as human beings.

Everything changes when you crack open your heart. In this book, you'll learn how to move through the four progressive openings: pain, compassion, connection, and love. It is in moving through these heart passages that true consciousness is revealed.

The second part of this book features the 365 Daily Illuminations, life-affirming messages that will guide you during the journey. Simply by reading the message for each day, you will easily move into joy and love.

978-1-935254-72-0, 192 pp., 6 x 9 $15.95

Becoming Your Best Self

The Guide to Clarity, Inspiration and Joy

What if you could receive Divine guidance at any time? What if you could clearly see your highest potential? What if you could heal the past, live in the present, and manifest your dreams in the future? In this delightfully inspiring book, Sara Wiseman teaches you how to establish a direct connection with the Divine that will raise your vibration, heal your heart, allow instant access to Universal information, and transform your life in the process.

Through step-by-step exercises you will learn a variety of life-changing skills—from attracting a soul mate to healing relationships to communicating with Divine guides and loved ones in spirit. Throughout, Wiseman shares simple yet profound messages that open the path to a new level of consciousness and to your own spiritual awakening.

978-0-7387-2794-3, 264 pp., 6 x 9 $16.95

Sara Wiseman

Your Psychic Child

How to Raise Intuitive & Spiritually Gifted Kids of All Ages

Want to take an active role in your child's psychic and spiritual development? This indispensable guide helps parents understand and nurture their uniquely gifted children.

Learn about the psychic awakening process and the talents that emerge with each age, from toddler to teen. Discover how to gently encourage your children to explore and develop their strengths in clairvoyance, energy healing and mediumship, and teach them how to connect with the Divine. Anchored in down-to-earth parental wisdom and alive with personal anecdotes, *Your Psychic Child* is an essential resource for parents who recognize their child's psychic and spiritual potential.

978-0-7387-2061-6, 312 pp., 6 x 9 $17.95

Writing the Divine

How to Use Channeling for Soul Growth & Healing

This amazing book shows you that learning channeling and channeled writing isn't just for gurus and psychics—it's as easy as closing your eyes and picking up your pen! In part one, Sara Wiseman shares clear, simple directions for divine receiving, how to use a journal for spiritual growth, and how to manifest in writing.

Part two invites you to experience directly the transformative power of The 33 Lessons, an inspiring collection of Divine lessons received by Wiseman, on love, life and spiritual awakening in this world.

978-0-7387-1581-0, 312 pp., 6 x 9 $16.95

Music by Martyrs of Sound

Sara Wiseman and Dr. Steve Koc create award-winning music with their band Martyrs of Sound. This music is ideal for meditation, prayer, yoga, massage, relaxation, insomnia, and healing, and is widely played on international airwaves.

Their albums include:

Mantra Chill Serene, luminous and healing mantra

Uncoiled Tribal dance trance for chakra opening from root to crown

Songs for Loving & Dying Tantric rock with a spiritual groove

Radhe's Dream Song of the Beloved, as expressed in healing mantra.

Listen and download at **www.martyrsofsound.com**

CPSIA information can be obtained at www.ICGtesting.com
Printed in the USA
LVOW121655010713

340893LV00001B/26/P

Intuition, Cancer & Miracles

A Passage of Hope & Healing

WITH DIVINE MESSAGES AND
MEDITATIONS FOR YOUR JOURNEY

SARA WISEMAN

NorLightsPress.com
762 State Road 458
Bedford IN 47421

Printed in the United States of America
ISBN: 978-1-935254-77-5

Cover Design by Leslie Venti
Book Design by Nadene Carter
Editing and collaboration by Sammie Justesen

First printing, 2013

Disclaimer

This book is not intended as a substitute for professional medical care. While this book supports the exploration of intuitive and spiritual methods of healing, it also recognizes the importance of traditional medicine, holistic medicine, and complementary therapies for healing and wellness.